PRAISE FOR

Forever: A Catholic Devotional for Your Marriage

"Jackie and Bobby's book is a prayerful and practical recipe for couples who want to grow in love for one another and God. Do your relationship a favor and read this book!"

—Marcel LeJeune, international Catholic speaker, author, and evangelist

"Saint John Paul II's theology of the body makes divine mystery accessible by speaking a language we can understand: the language of our bodies. Jackie and Bobby Angel do the same thing: by illuminating practical, concrete, and incarnational ways to live in love with your spouse, they bring this awe-inspiring teaching into the everyday of married life."

—Stephanie Calis, author, *Invited: The Ultimate Catholic Wedding Planner*, and Co-Founder, Spoken Bride

"In a time where common sense grows increasingly less common, this book is a sage, practical guide for couples to grow in holiness and true intimacy. Jackie and Bobby have given couples a road map to sexual freedom and marital joy sharing practical insights and timeless wisdom with each turn of the page. This book—like its authors—is a true gift to the Church and one that will bless your current or upcoming marriage."

—Mark Hart, Executive Vice President of Life Teen International, best-selling author, speaker, radio host

FOREVER

A Catholic Devotional
for Your Marriage

By Jackie Francois Angel and Bobby Angel

Foreword by Bill Donaghy

BOOKS & MEDIA
Boston

Library of Congress Cataloging-in-Publication Data

Names: Angel, Jackie Francois, author.

Title: Forever : a Catholic devotional for your marriage / by Jackie Francois Angel and Bobby Angel.

Description: Boston : Pauline Books & Media, 2017.

Identifiers: LCCN 2016058215| ISBN 9780819827432 (pbk.) | ISBN 0819827436 (pbk.)

Subjects: LCSH: Married people--Prayers and devotions. | Catholic Church--Prayers and devotions. | John Paul II, Pope, 1920-2005. Theology of the body.

Classification: LCC BX2170.M3 A54 2017 | DDC 242/.644--dc23

LC record available at https://lccn.loc.gov/2016058215

The Scripture quotations contained herein are from the *New Revised Standard Version Bible: Catholic Edition*, copyright © 1989, 1993, Division of Christian Education of the National Council of the Churches of Christ in the United States of America. Used by permission. All rights reserved.

Excerpts from the English translation of the *Catechism of the Catholic Church* for use in the United States of America, copyright © 1994, United States Catholic Conference, Inc. — Libreria Editrice Vaticana. Used with permission.

Excerpts from papal and magisterium texts copyright © Libreria Editrice Vaticana. All rights reserved. Used with permission.

The Four Loves by C. S. Lewis, copyright © C. S. Lewis Pte. Ltd. 1960. Extract reprinted by permission.

Cover photo by Kristin Rogers

Published by Pauline Books & Media, 50 Saint Paul's Avenue, Boston, MA 02130-3491

Printed in the U.S.A.

www.pauline.org

Pauline Books & Media is the publishing house of the Daughters of St. Paul, an international congregation of women religious serving the Church with the communications media.

1 2 3 4 5 6 7 8 9   21 20 19 18 17

Contents

WEEK ONE
Why Am I Here?

WEEK TWO
What Is Love?

WEEK THREE
What Is Marriage?

WEEK FOUR
How Can Our Love Last?

What Endangers Our Love?

WEEK SIX

What Is God's Plan for Our Family?

Foreword

You are holding an absolute gem in your hands.

For starters, this book is a crisp, readable, and very thorough walk through the beautiful vision of the theology of the body, Saint John Paul II's epic meditation on what it means to be a human person. You and I were loved, gifted, and called into existence by God to become loving gifts in return.

But this book does so much more than deliver rich dogma—it's a devotional! Each reflection is beautifully crafted for your prayerful meditation, ends with an invitation to live out the teaching it expounded upon, and then closes with a prayer. It's basically one-stop shopping for married couples to know, love, and live out the theology of the body in this age of radical self-centeredness. Through its daily explanations of the theology of the body, it reveals how a couple can discover our amazing human capacity for self-giving love.

As a personal friend of Bobby and Jackie, it has been a huge grace to see their hearts grow in friendship and mutual love and now step into the dance that is marriage and family, the earthly sign of the Great Dance to which every human heart is invited.

How refreshing to hear their stories and to see how they have learned and continue to learn the steps in this dance as they prepare for their ultimate entrance into the heart of the Bridegroom himself. In this age of varied interpretations of marriage, sexuality, masculinity, and femininity, this little work brings a clarity that is sorely needed. The sign of our masculinity and femininity is indeed of divine design. So take up this gem of a book, fellow married lovers! Treasure it and let its wisdom and light be a source of God's grace for you, your marriage, and, through that holy love, a light for the world to see.

BILL DONAGHY

Introduction

Every person on this earth is united in more ways than one: we all breathe air, we all need water, we all love nachos (most of us), and we all have an insatiable need to love and be loved. Without love, human existence quickly loses its color, its vitality, and its meaning. Because love is so key to our happiness, we often find unhealthy ways to satisfy our ache for love, and sometimes we try to repress or deny its existence altogether. But our longing for love always returns. You could say that it's built into our very creation as man and woman.

It was a celibate pope, of all people, who helped us to understand the mysterious dynamic of love: Saint John Paul II.

John Paul II is like a spiritual grandfather to the both of us. We spent the first two decades of our lives under his pontificate. And what a pope to grow up with! His joy and charisma were infectious, and we watched with excitement as he travel the globe.

Even as he aged and grew ill, John Paul II still carried a charismatic light of holiness that sparked hope in others. We both cried when he passed away on April 2, 2005. We felt we had lost someone we knew personally, someone we loved and who also loved us. We were also grateful that he was free of his trials and sufferings and that he would finally be completely united with God, his heart's lover.

Along with God's providential guiding hand, we credit the teachings of John Paul II (and possibly his direct intercession) for bringing us together as a couple. We were on different vocational journeys when we met at a retreat dedicated to comprehending and living out this pope's great body of work known today as *Man and Woman He Created Them: A Theology of the Body* (henceforth *TOB*). From this seemingly random encounter, a friendship and eventually a romantic relationship blossomed. Now married, we are amazed at how God used one saint above all others to form us intellectually and spiritually and to lead us to a deeper love of God, the Author of all life, who is Love itself.

Through John Paul II's great work we received a new "lens" through which to see the world. We began to understand how God revealed his divine plan of love in our bodies, in our creation as male and female. We began to understand that what we do to our bodies we do to our souls. This carries weight especially for those of us called to the great vocation of marriage.

In generations to come, as the Church looks back, it will likely see John Paul II as a brave shepherd whose teachings gave clarity to so many lost in the cultural wasteland of the sexual revolution. We have seen the power of this great teaching in our lives and how it has changed others, which is why we're so eager to pass it on.

John Paul II's great vision of the human person is not secret Gnostic information or anything truly *new* to Christianity. Understanding what it means to be incarnate—to be bodily—is at the heart of Christianity, but we have all been influenced by a modernist perspective that sees the human body as something only outside of our *real* selves, a mere tool to be enhanced, reshaped, or even discarded. We've lost the right way to truly see our bodies.

John Paul II had his finger on the pulse of modern culture and saw where it was headed, so he packaged an ancient vision of the integrated human person in a way that would make sense to our modern ears. We are more than random biological cells and neurons chaotically firing together, he declared. Our bodies are worth *infinitely more* than a hook-up or a one-night-stand. Our bodies, so often misunderstood, actually contain a grand theology (a study of God)! The *invisible* mystery of God is physically manifest in the *visible* sign of the human body.

But how can we adequately learn this amazingly rich teaching and apply it to our lives? First, we must be *open* to receiving this great truth. Like Christ himself, John Paul II never *imposes* the truth—he only *proposes*. For those of us who have grown up Catholic or within a Christian tradition, we particularly need to hear the story of God's love for us with new ears and to have an open attitude willing both to wrestle with God intellectually and to allow him to gently transform our hearts. If we have come out of poor marriages or relationships that have wounded us deeply, we need to open our hearts up to God's great love story all the more. Only he can heal the ache of our hearts.

So many couples we encounter ask us, "*Where* was this teaching twenty years ago!" or they say sadly, "We never heard any of this." To those couples we say, "It's *never* too late. Give thanks that you're finally *hearing* it!" God meets us in our brokenness and leads us out toward wholeness. So many wounded people starve for love in the world, our workplaces, our homes; we need to receive this good news and to be missionaries of love to the world.

To those couples who learn this teaching at the beginning of their dating relationships: brothers and sisters, we have the profound *responsibility* to be witnesses of this life-giving and joyful love for a world *starving* for authentic love. We've grown up in a culture of promiscuity that degrades the human body. We need to reclaim the conversation and witness to the joy and radiance that a devoted marriage can offer to the world.

For married couples, we hope this book will help you pray with your spouse, as well as grow in your understanding of this profound vision from John Paul II. We also hope that you will find joy in the vocation of marriage and discover how we can make the love of God physically present in the world through the simple act of loving our spouse and our children. We need holy husbands and holy wives, holy fathers and holy mothers. Because marriage is an emotional, intellectual, physical, and spiritual union, this path begins by praying together and uniting yourselves spiritually with one another.

We were blessed to begin our marriage with this formational teaching, and we pray the insights of this great saint will bless you as they have blessed us. We are humbled to be messengers of this teaching and to be missionaries in the service of Jesus Christ and his Church. We have all been made for a love that lasts *forever* and there's no better time to begin this journey than today.

Saint John Paul II, pray for us!

How to Use This Book

The primary purpose of this book is to lead couples into prayer and meditation on the glory of God's love and his call to love freely, totally, faithfully, and fruitfully.

We also hope to give you an overview of Saint John Paul II's teaching on the theology of the body and lead you through the major themes in this beautiful body of work. If you are already familiar with the theology of the body, we hope this book will bring you some new insights and ways to live it out as a couple.

We read several books as an engaged couple that helped us to grow together intellectually and spiritually, including Fulton Sheen's *Three to Get Married*, Saint John Paul II's document "On the Christian Family in the Modern World" (*Familiaris Consortio*), and other great books on the theology of the body. This is why we believe in the power of doing spiritual reading together as a couple.

The challenges in this book focus on married couples, but it will be helpful for couples who are dating and engaged as well. At whatever stage you may be in your relationship, we hope this devotional will help you grow in your relationship. Feel free to read the chapters together as a couple or on your own. But be sure to *talk* about it afterward if you are able. Communicate with one another about what moved or challenged you—it will be time well spent.

It is possible to read this book straight through, but we hope you will take the time to meditate and reflect on the daily topic and allow for a six-week devotion (trust us, there's plenty to chew on; it will take a lifetime to unpack some of these themes!). Reading a book, especially a good book, is never a race.

We hope you take the time to read this book *prayerfully*. Before you read, ask God to reveal what he wants you to learn. Daily prompts and challenges will help you along the journey. Don't be afraid to sit with whatever is stirred up by the readings. None of us have lived chastity perfectly, and the theology of the body can bring to the surface past memories, failures, and deep wounds. But the message of Christ is always a message of hope and redemption. No one is ever "too far gone" to return to the welcoming arms of God the Father. To repeat the constant refrain of our favorite saint: "Be not afraid!"

You may want to pick a favorite feast day or a Marian feast to start or end your devotional reading. The intercession of our Holy Mother and the saints can only unite couples more in Christ.

We hope this book helps you to grow as a couple. John Paul II and his teachings changed our lives. His writings have been studied and disseminated by scholars, speakers, writers, and many talented individuals; we are humbled to also share this great teaching with others.

Have fun, and remember to laugh with your spouse. If nothing else, this book will make a worthy coaster for your coffee.

Praised be Jesus Christ!

WEEK ONE

Why Am I Here?

~

Day One

The Meaning of Life

Why am I here?

What's the meaning of my life?

Do I have a purpose?

These questions have provoked and plagued humanity since the time of the ancient philosophers. Today, the multiplication of self-help books and therapist offices suggest that we are not any closer to knowing the purpose of our existence.

But maybe we've *already* been given the answer. Maybe we just need to rediscover it or see it with new eyes.

Our answers to life's important questions largely direct our energies and choices. For many centuries, it was commonly understood that there was a divine design behind all of creation—whether it was attributed to the Greek gods; the Egyptian deities; the God of Abraham, Isaac, and Jacob; or Jesus Christ himself. Centuries before our current millennium, advances in science and modern philosophies led many to ditch the idea of an all-loving God designing the universe (or at the very least demote him to the position of an aloof "clockmaker" content to wind up creation and never interfere with it again).

When we believe that we are simply the result of random biological processes and chance, our lives lack meaning. This can be crushing. These ideas have left a great void in the human heart. We're facing a societal spiritual crisis. Violence, promiscuity, and suicide rates have all been increasing steadily. People have access to a global network of communication, information, and opportunities, but they are more depressed and bored than ever before.

You may have felt the weight of this "crisis of existence." You may wonder what this life is all about. You may question where this ache for meaning comes from and how it can possibly be answered.

Thankfully, we have not been left alone. We've been given a saint to guide us. Saint John Paul II formed himself so closely to the heart of Christ that he could sense the wayward signs of the times. So he devoted his energies to leading the stray sheep back to the heart of the Father who has willed us into existence and had us in mind before the dawn of creation itself.

The secret to our existence is closer than we realize. To find the secret of life we don't need another self-help book or to see a guru atop a Himalayan mountain.

The answer to this ache is written right into our bodies.

Daily Challenge

Think about your life up to this point and consider everything (good and bad) that has brought you to where you are now. Can you feel a sense of direction or see a purpose in the events in your life and why they have happened as they have? Discuss this with your spouse.

Prayer

Lord, help us to find in you the meaning of our existence and the answer to the ache of our heart for purpose. Thank you for bringing us to where we are today, and be with us in the days ahead. Protect and guide our vocation so we can truly love one another. Amen.

***

Day Two

Back to the Beginning

If you've ever picked up a book and flipped open to a random page and started reading, it can be pretty confusing. Names, places, and plot developments mean little to nothing because you have no context for the greater story taking place.

With any great story, you must start at the beginning. Saint John Paul II embarks on his teaching with the prompt Jesus himself gave to the Pharisees who challenged him on marriage. He called them to look back to the beginning:

> Have you not read that the one who made them at the beginning "made them male and female," and said, "For this reason a man shall leave his father and mother and be joined to his wife, and the two shall become one flesh"? (Mt 19:8)

The "beginning" refers to Genesis, the scriptural account of our earthly creation, where we see that God created the world *out of love*, since God himself *is love* (see 1 Jn 4:8). God's love is creative and overflowing. In this story of creation, we encounter God who is Love, and by nature love diffuses itself; it flows out like water from a fountain.

Thus, *all* creation is for the glory of God and reveals his Truth, Beauty, and Goodness. The stars, fish of the sea, creeping things, and wild animals are all God's handiwork; all of them are called "good." But, as everything in the order of creation gets more beautiful and more complex, God saved the best for last:

us. He created us male and female and doesn't call us just "good," but "very good," since we alone are created in his image and likeness—the image and likeness of *love*. In this profound truth we find our purpose—*to love and to be loved*.

Saint Teresa of Kolkata often emphasized that we are not just numbers in the world but that we all have been created to love and to be loved by God in return.

The book of Genesis is a profound narrative detailing the creation of man and woman in the image and likeness of God. The first book of the Scriptures lays the foundation for the story of the human person who is created out of God's generosity and is destined to share in that blessed union of love.

Is this not the desire of every human heart?

Daily Challenge

What are some ways your spouse shows you love? How do you show yours in return? Read the first chapter of Genesis slowly and take the time to absorb its poetic language and imagery. Discuss it with your spouse. What new insights come to mind?

Prayer

God, open our eyes to see the way we are loved each day by you and by others. Allow our love to always reach outward and not to remain within ourselves. Amen.

❧

DAY THREE

God Knocks on Our Hearts

Our purpose is to love and to be loved, which is why the human heart fears few things as much as loneliness. Knowing this, we can understand why the ache of Adam was so deep. In the second account of the creation story in Genesis 2, Adam cannot find a suitable partner among the other animals. He quickly realizes that none of the animals can be his partner. He cannot cuddle with the porcupine, and the giraffe proves an ill-suited dance partner. Profoundly alone, Adam longs for life-giving love.

We can probably relate to Adam's loneliness. Whether loneliness strikes in marriage or a new community, work environment or even in a crowded room, this aloneness seems part of the human condition. While we may be tempted to just cry and belt out a rendition of "All by Myself" or "Somebody to Love," these times of loneliness can be opportunities to draw closer to God. By our solitude, we are "set into a *unique, exclusive, and unrepeatable relationship with God himself*" (*TOB* 6:2).

A priest-friend once told us that, "Loneliness is simply God knocking on your heart, asking you to spend time with him." We often think of loneliness as the enemy, as a terrible threat to our peace and happiness. Instead loneliness is perhaps a plea from God to remember him and to turn to him first before we try to fill up our lives with any other person or thing.

Solitude is not the same thing as loneliness. Times of solitude are set aside purposefully for reading, prayer, or simply to be alone. Today, because we are glued to our cell phones and caught up in the endless distractions they provide, we are often never truly silent. And thus we risk not hearing the still, small voice of God. It is not good for us to be alone, but once we realize that in him "we live and move and have our being" (Acts 17:28), we are never truly alone.

All of us, without exception, have the "ache of Adam," this fundamental ache within our being for wholeness—a cry for *communion*.

God wants to satisfy that longing.

Daily Challenge

Find time to be alone. Turn off your phone or leave it far away from you. Sit outside if you can. Listen to your breathing and observe God's creation. Ask for peace in this moment.

Prayer

God, help us to seek solitude so that we may see and hear you. Help us to reclaim an appreciation for silence and your presence all around us. In you we live, move, and have our being (see Acts 17:28). Amen.

༄

DAY FOUR

Waking Up to Love

> Then the LORD God said, "It is not good that the man should be alone; I will make him a helper as his partner." (Gen 2:18)

Middle school dances are wonderfully awkward. At the height of puberty, when girls tower over boys who barely reach their shoulders, warring parties are subjected to the bizarre cultural ritual of *dance*.

Some of us remember these dances like they were yesterday. A brave male and female eventually emerge from their respective corners of the room and begin the uncoordinated sway that leads others to the dance floor. Maybe you were the self-conscious wreck who detested having to deal with the other sex, or maybe you were the life of the party. Or maybe you were the kid who had a mega-crush on a certain someone since kindergarten (whose name you can *still* remember) and you got googly eyes whenever you saw them.

If you've ever experienced that feeling (whether as an adolescent or as an adult) when you see a beautiful person across the room who takes your breath away, you have a tiny glimpse of what Adam saw in Eve.

"At last!" he cries out. "This at last is bone of my bones and flesh of my flesh" (Gen 2:23). With wonder and fascination, Adam exclaims, *"Look, a body that expresses the 'person'!"* (*TOB*

14:4). The body of Eve, a woman, awakens Adam's understanding that he has an "other," another being just like him. Being of Adam's rib—his very bones—signified the whole person in the Jewish understanding.

This unity transforms the solitude we *all* experience into a purposeful communion with another person. We're meant for union, and our bodies express this fact. Male and female bodies only make sense in light of one another. We are made for each other. And this communion with an earthly person ultimately points us to communion with God.

Sometimes spouses refer to one another as "my other half," or to lovers as "two pieces of a whole." There's some truth to these expressions for they echo the reality that we come from a common place. The unity of man and woman is "based on masculinity and femininity, which are, as it were, two different 'incarnations' ... [of] the same human being, created 'in the image of God'" (*TOB* 8:1).

While Genesis uses figurative language, it points us to the deeper truth of our creation—we are made in the image of God who is love and a communion of distinct persons: Father, Son, and Holy Spirit. "Man becomes an image of God not so much in the moment of solitude as in the moment of communion" (*TOB* 9:3).

Adam does not truly become himself until he sees himself in relation to Eve. Think of a middle-school boy totally self-absorbed until he is awakened by the beauty of a female classmate. His whole world changes!

The waking up we all experience through the eyes of love can be a profound event. Whether during middle school, college, or well into adulthood, being love-struck calls us out of ourselves and into relationship with another, which is exactly what we were created for.

Daily Challenge

Recall the first time you saw your spouse. What went through your mind? What feelings emerged in your heart? How would you describe the first sensation of feeling "in love"?

Prayer

O God, help us to constantly ignite a holy fascination and wonder for one another. Thank you, Lord, for bringing us together in this union so that we might not be alone, but may journey together to our ultimate destination: your love in heaven. Amen.

꩜

DAY FIVE

The Human Heart's Deepest Desire

> The gaze, the eye, is even more important than sex to enter into communion.[1]

In preparing for marriage, our minds often wander to the wedding night and we imagine seeing one another naked. Why is that?

Obviously, we desire to be physically united to our beloved and it's hard to do that wearing clothing. We feel passion and a burning desire *to be one* with our spouse. But more than a physical act or the mere absence of clothing, the nakedness of our bodies is another sign of how God has created us to love.

Man and woman, Saint John Paul II writes, "see and know each other, in fact, with all the peace of the interior gaze, which creates precisely the fullness of the intimacy of persons" (*TOB* 13:1). Our naked bodies signify the deeper reality of a total abandonment in the arms of our beloved. Bodily nakedness is not a minor detail then for John Paul II's great teaching; our nakedness has great spiritual significance.

Nakedness implies vulnerability, simplicity, and even freedom. Depending on our upbringing, though, our understanding

---

1. Raniero Cantalamessa, OFM, *Contemplating the Trinity: The Path to Abundant Christian Life* (Frederick, MD: Word Among Us Press, 2007), 100.

of the human body may be colored by a distorted, puritanical version of Christianity that is ashamed of the naked body. In the beginning, however, "the man and his wife were both naked, and were not ashamed" (Gen 2:25).

As John Paul II reflects, "The fact that 'they did not feel shame' means that the woman was not an 'object' for the man, nor he for her'" (*TOB* 19:1). Lust had not yet entered the picture because it was the result of the first sin of pride and disobedience. Thus, Adam and Eve could see each other in all their naked glory without feeling a desire to use the other for pleasure. They saw each other's true dignity as persons made in the image and likeness of God, revealing his beauty and goodness.

According to Saint Augustine, the deepest desire of the human heart is to really *see* another person and to be seen and loved in return.[2] We can be naked and seen not just physically, but also emotionally and spiritually. Spiritual nakedness and vulnerability are just as essential to marriage as bodily nakedness. Nothing is held back, nothing is kept secret. All is revealed to the one who has vowed to love us totally—in all our weaknesses, strengths, quirks, and oddities. This is real intimacy—or as the sound of the word suggests, "in-to-me-see"—when someone can see all of who we are and still love us.

When we lay down our defenses and emotional barriers, we embrace the fullness of the other person, in good times and bad. None of us wants to be loved only at our best—we also want to be loved at our worst.

---

2. See Saint Augustine, Sermon 69, c. 2, 3.

Daily Challenge

Take an "in-to-me-see" challenge. Look into your spouse's eyes for four minutes without distractions. Set a timer and look into his or her eyes without turning away. See what happens. Do you laugh? Do you cry? Are you grateful?

Prayer

God, help us to see the beauty and goodness of each other in all our strengths and weaknesses. As Adam and Eve were "naked without shame" in the garden, give us the grace to not fear being vulnerable with one another. Amen.

❧

Day Six

In the Image of a Gift

Why do people love giving and receiving gifts? Sometimes we stress over finding the perfect gift for our beloved during the holidays, or we worry about what to give a friend for an upcoming birthday, graduation, or wedding. But the moment of gift-giving often brings pure delight—for the receiver *and* the giver.

But *why* do we bother giving gifts? Is it nothing more than custom? Or is the act of giving buried more deeply in the human heart than we realize?

One of the key words in the great vision Saint John Paul II laid out, a word he returns to again and again, is *gift*. Why? God's free outpouring of love into creation and into each one of us is a gift and—amazingly—God desires the human person to participate in this dynamic of gift-giving.

> God has revealed his innermost secret: God himself is an eternal exchange of love, Father, Son, and Holy Spirit, and he has destined us to share in that exchange. (*CCC* 221)

As Venerable Fulton Sheen wrote, "It takes three to make love . . . If there is only one God, whom does he love? He loves his Son, and that mutual love is the Holy Spirit."[3] From this eternal exchange of love between the lover (Father) and the beloved (Son)

---

3. Fulton Sheen, *Three to Get Married* (New York: Scepter Publishers, Inc, 1996), 52.

proceeds another Person (the Holy Spirit). A husband and wife *mirror* this exchange of love and, if it is God's will, new life can result from their intimate union.

God is not an old man sitting in the clouds, but a dynamic union of Three Persons in one God. This *dynamic of love* present within the Trinity is the reason we have been created, and this is why love—and only love—can satisfy our aching hearts. Made *in the image and likeness of love*, the human being is "the highest expression" of God's "divine gift, because he bears within himself the inner dimension of the gift" (*TOB* 19:3).

This great mystery of love, God's innermost secret, is naturally revealed through our bodies, male and female. John Paul II calls this the "spousal meaning" of the body. The spouses' ability to freely give and receive love mirrors the exchange of love within God himself. The human body has the "*power to express love: precisely that love in which the human person becomes a gift* and—through this gift—fulfills the very meaning of his being and existence" (*TOB* 15:1).

We love gift-giving because we have been created in the image of a gift! We can never discover our potential and the fullness of our humanity without living this reality: Man, according to a well-known phrase from the Vatican II document "Pastoral Constitution on the Church in the Modern World" (*Gaudium et Spes*), "cannot fully find himself except through a sincere gift of himself."[4]

---

4. *Gaudium et Spes*, Vatican Website, December 7, 1965, no. 24, accessed Nov. 3, 2016, http://www.vatican.va/archive/hist_councils/ii_vatican_council/documents/vat-ii_const_19651207_gaudium-et-spes_en.html.

Daily Challenge

Talk to your spouse about the greatest gift you ever received. Perhaps it was a cherished memento from someone you loved, a vacation, or maybe even a child. Why was it so meaningful?

Prayer

O God, help us to appreciate the gift of your love in our lives and the gift of our spouse. Give us the grace to love unselfishly as you love us. Amen.

Day Seven

The Wedding Feast of Heaven

Reading the Bible can seem like a daunting endeavor. Even though we may hear the readings proclaimed at every Mass, most of us are intimidated by talk of cubits, bizarre culinary laws, and difficult-to-pronounce names. Even if we are very familiar with Scripture, we can still be at a loss for words when pressed to explain what the Bible is *actually* trying to say.

At the start of this week, we reflected on God's creation of the world and how "in the beginning" he created us male and female in his image and likeness. This love between husband and wife—the ecstasy of their union—is a mere foretaste of the end, the ecstasy we are meant to experience in heaven, where we will be united to God who is love.

It's no mistake that the Bible starts with a wedding and ends with a wedding. The marriage between Adam and Eve in Genesis points us to (and is a foretaste of) the even *greater* marriage in the book of Revelation (the last book of the Bible). But the marriage Revelation speaks about is in heaven—the marriage between Jesus, the Bridegroom, and us, the Church, the radiant bride. The wedding feast of heaven is *our* wedding—the wedding and marriage that last *forever*. Thus, the purpose of the Bible from beginning to end is to tell God's great love story with us. God is calling us to communion with him in heaven.

The *Catechism of the Catholic Church* affirms this call to communion: "Only in God will [man] find the truth and happiness he never stops searching for: The dignity of man rests above all on the fact that he is called to communion with God" (27).

Now, if our concept of heaven is one of infinite boredom where we are fanning Jesus with palm branches and feeding him grapes for all eternity, then, yes, we may not get excited about "communion with God." However, if we *really* know that God not only loves us, but that he would also rather die than spend eternity without us, we would tremble in wonder and awe. It is truly miraculous that God proposes his love to us, a love that longs to be in an "eternal exchange of love" (*CCC* 221).

If we have been disappointed in romance or are cynical about the notion of eternal love, we must remember that *only* in God will we find the truth and happiness we have been searching for our whole lives. Even as we journey toward heaven with our spouse as a "helpmate," we only love because God loved us first (see 1 Jn 4:19).

Authentic love, something we will examine next week, never seeks to use, abuse, or wound. Love, as God intended, sets us free and *is* humanly possible, but it takes work and purification to achieve. While always imperfect here on earth, love itself comes from God and, when lived rightly, draws us back to him.

Daily Challenge

Discuss with your spouse how your thoughts on heaven have changed throughout your life. Read 1 Peter 1:3–9 together and share what stands out most to you.

Prayer

O God, help us to understand that you created us out of love, by love, and for love, and that you long to share eternity with us. Help us to love as you love. Be with us as we move through this devotional. Open our hearts to receive this great vision. Amen.

WEEK TWO

What Is Love?

Day One

I Love Nachos and I Love You

When pressed to answer the question, "What is love?" most people today (if they don't break out in song first) would say it's "a feeling" or "a strong emotion."

It doesn't help that in the English language we have only one word for this phenomenon of "love." With the same breath we utter, "I love nachos," or "I love my Sriracha," or "I love my phone," or even "I love my spouse."

Can you really love your spouse the same way you love Sriracha? Or nachos? For some of us, yes—we love our spouse with the same passion we love nachos. But that's not the point. In English we are limited to *one word* to describe a whole spectrum of attachment and profound devotion.

Life can get messy when we're unclear about the type of affection we're trying to convey. Miscommunication over the nature of our love toward another can cause a lot of heartache. If one significant other says, "I love you," meaning, "I really like you and enjoy hanging out with you like a buddy," but the other responds, "I love you," and means, "I want to spend the rest of my life with you and have your babies," well . . . that can create some problems!

Feelings can get the best of us and cause us to say something we think we mean but don't really understand. Sometimes we say we are "in love," but we might actually be more enamored with the feeling of infatuation or the pleasure a person gives us than with the actual person we claim to love.

Luckily for us, the ancient Greeks distinguished the varying forms and degrees of love and used four different words that can help us understand this phenomenon of love:

⊕ *Storge*

⊕ *Philia*

⊕ *Eros*

⊕ *Agape*

As the week goes on, we will look at each of these degrees of love and how they play out in our lives. From our discussion in Week One, it's important to remember that we were made *in the image and likeness of God who is love*. Love is much more profound than a mere feeling or a fleeting emotion. Love, in its highest form, is the driving element behind our creation and it is why we are restless when a lesser love proves unsatisfying.

Above all, love is a profound *choice*. Love is faithful through thick and thin, for richer or poorer, in sickness and in health. Love chooses to desire greatness for the other person and feels a sense of responsibility for him or her.

Along with theology of the body concepts, this week we will also be drawing from some writings of Pope Benedict XVI and

The Four Loves, a book written by the beloved British atheist-turned-apologist C. S. Lewis.

You may realize as you read that the love you have experienced in life has often been wanting. But this is no reason to grow bitter or anxious. As John Paul II reassures us in his book *Love and Responsibility*, "There is no need to be discouraged that this [love] happens sometimes in intricate and convoluted ways. Grace has the power to make straight the ways of human love."[1]

Daily Challenge

Ask your spouse if he or she has ever struggled to be "on the same page" with another person's love in a past relationship. Why do you think it's so hard for love to be communicated effectively?

Prayer

O Lord my God,
teach my heart this day where and how to see you,
where and how to find you.
Let me seek you in my desire,
let me desire you in my seeking.
Let me find you by loving you,
let me love you when I find you.[2]

---

1. Karol Wojtyla, *Love and Responsibility*, trans. Grzegorz Ignatik (Boston: Pauline Books & Media, 2013), 122.

2. Anselm of Canterbury, *Proslogion*, 1.

༄

DAY TWO

A Love of Choice

We all know that a kiss of affection between family members is not the same as a kiss between lovers (although, lovers can have kisses of affection). You don't kiss your weird, hairy uncle with the same passion that you kiss your spouse (our apologies if your spouse may be weird and hairy). We know at an instinctive level that love has different stages or dimensions.

Storge (*STOR-gay*) is an affection-type of love, a feeling of empathy based on fondness or familiarity. It's the love we see between parents and children or between other family members. You may never have been friends with a sibling, cousin, or uncle outside of the context of being related to them, but *storge* is a fondness that comes with familiarity—and it can exist even if you can't stand someone!

Even animals experience affection between one another (which is why we love odd animal pairings and cat videos on the internet). But affection isn't the highest form of love; it's the love that *least* separates us from other creatures.

Philia (*FIL-ee-uh*), on the other hand, is a love of choice. You've heard forms of the word before—think of Philadelphia, the "City of Brotherly Love." The root word "*philos*" means beloved, dear, friendly. *Philia* is true friendship love; it is the love of a real friend, not simply a work colleague, a classmate, or a bowling buddy.

Friendship, as C. S. Lewis puts it, is "the least natural of loves; the least instinctive, organic, biological, gregarious, and necessary. . . . The species, biologically considered, has no need of it."[3]

Lewis isn't knocking friendship; far from it. He is merely pointing out that, while our species needs some sort of affection to clan together, to desire to procreate, we don't *need* friendship to survive. But we're not animals. We are human persons created out of love. So while friendship may serve no practical purpose, true friendship makes life worth living.

In discovering a new friend, we often feel a joyful shock. We think, "Wow, there is someone else who is like me. I thought I was the only one!" Whether it's a shared love of zombie movies, classical music, or Canadian curling, friendship often happens when we experience a unique bond with another person that enriches our lives.

There are different kinds of friendship. Aristotle named three forms of friendship: utility, pleasure, and virtue. A friendship of utility is based on function or use (think casual work relationships), and a friendship of pleasure is based on shared experiences (love of music, exercise, or bungee-jumping). But the most complete friendship is a virtuous. In a virtuous friendship, there is a common goal in which both people encourage one another to excellence. In a virtuous Christian friendship, the common goal is heaven and a life of virtue.

To be truly friends with your spouse is a great gift. Many modern couples slide into a relationship after being physically

3. C. S. Lewis, *The Four Loves* (New York: Mariner Books, 2012), 58.

intimate, only later to realize that they were never friends to begin with. "We picture lovers face to face," Lewis notes, "but friends side by side; their eyes look ahead."[4]

True friendship between spouses doesn't make another person into an idol. Spouses who are friends walk together in the same direction, supporting one another along the journey. Married friends are able to converse over things that matter and share laughter and faith, which is a great gift. And a virtuous friendship within marriage leads to the greatest gift of all: heaven.

Daily Challenge

Share with your spouse an example of a friendship of utility or pleasure that you have had at some point in your life. Discuss a common goal (or goals) in your own relationship that unites you both in a virtuous friendship.

Prayer

Lord, thank you for our families and the *storge* love that exists between us. Heal any broken bonds between family members, especially if one of us played a role in a strained relationship. Thank you for all the friendships in our lives—may you be a part of them all. And thank you for our relationship, for our romance and friendship. May we continue to journey together to heaven.

---

4. Ibid.

৯৯

Day Three

The True, Good, and Beautiful

We all know what *eros* (*AIR-ohs*) feels like. If you are a living, breathing man or woman with blood flowing through your veins, you have experienced *eros*.

While we get the modern word "erotic" from the Greek word *eros*, the word *eros* has a much fuller meaning. Saint John Paul II wrote that *eros* is that "inner power that 'attracts' man to the true, the good, and the beautiful" (*TOB* 47:5).

Eros prompts a young man to drive across the country from Florida to pursue a California girl (which is exactly what happened in our own love story). *Eros* is ultimately the *yearning* for the true, good, and beautiful that calls us out of ourselves. It might be found in the beauty of a sunset, or a song that moves us to tears, or in a truth that pierces our hearts, or an act of kindness for someone who is hungry or thirsty.

Within marriage, *eros* draws us to all that is true, good, and beautiful in the beloved, not just the pleasure he or she can give. *Eros* is not lust. But the force of *eros* can be twisted for our own self-serving pleasure, which often happens in our fallen world.

Pope Benedict XVI noted in "God Is Love" (*Deus Caritas Est*): "*Eros* needs to be disciplined and purified if it is to provide not just a fleeting pleasure, but also a certain foretaste of the pinnacle of our existence, of that beatitude for which our whole being yearns."[5] As we learned last week, that "beatitude for which our whole being yearns" is heaven, where love lasts forever and we will experience the fullness of the good, true, and beautiful. Each sacramental marriage is supposed to be a foretaste of this fullness.

However, since *eros* is so powerful, there's always the danger of being in love with pleasure itself. Or we may fall in love with the *idea* of someone rather than the actual person. Passion can also easily be mistaken for a long-lasting "until-death-do-us-part" love. But when we mistake the impassioned feelings of *eros* for a fully mature love, we can get ourselves (and our relationships) in trouble, because when the same passion is no longer present, we assume that we no longer love the person.

When *eros* is directed correctly it loves the true, the good, and the beautiful within the other person. But the fulfillment of our love is never in *eros* alone. While we ache to capture the beauty of a sunset or a song, we know we can never stay in that moment of beauty forever—not on this side of eternity, at least.

God wants to take us deeper into the mystery of his love. Believe it or not, God actually has an *eros* for man! He desires us with the ardent love that moves from the divine energy of *eros* to the highest of all loves, which we will consider about tomorrow: *agape* love.

5. Benedict XVI, *Deus Caritas Est*, Vatican Web site, December 25, 2005, no. 4, accessed Nov. 3, 2016, http://w2.vatican.va/content/benedict-xvi/en/encyclicals/documents/hf_ben-xvi_enc_ 20051225_deus-caritas-est.html.

Daily Challenge

Discuss a moment or two in your life when you experienced a beauty, truth, or goodness so profound that you just wanted to stay there forever. Do you remember a time when you felt an ache and yearning in your heart? What or who did you search for to satisfy this ache?

Prayer

God, thank you for this burning desire in our bodies, hearts, minds, and souls for the beautiful, good, and true. Help us, especially when we feel this ache and longing, to turn to you and to pray:

> O God, you are my God, I seek you,
> my soul thirsts for you;
> my flesh faints for you,
> as in a dry and weary land where there is no water.
> So I have looked upon you in the sanctuary,
> beholding your power and glory.
> Because your steadfast love is better than life,
> my lips will praise you.
> So I will bless you as long as I live;
> I will lift up my hands and call on your name.

Psalm 63

⁊

Day Four

When Agape Love Blooms

No one has greater love than this, to lay down one's life for one's friends. (Jn 15:13)

Even if we've never studied this last type of love, *agape* (*uh-GAH-pay*), we have all heard or seen examples of it in our lives. They may be few and far between, but when we see *agape* love in action, it inspires and moves us to love more deeply.

We saw this *agape* love in a relationship between mutual friends (names have been changed). Sam was a strapping, handsome, and humble man who pursued the lovely and kind-hearted Kristy. While they were dating, Kristy was diagnosed with an advanced stage of cancer. As she started chemotherapy, this healthy, athletic woman became more and more frail, losing her hair and even having to use a wheelchair. While many men would have left a sick and dying woman, Sam did not. Instead of saying, "Goodbye," because Kristy was in a situation he had not signed up for, Sam said to her, "I want to love you in good times and bad, in sickness and in health, till death do us part. Will you marry me?"

Of course she said yes. And as Sam loved and cared for Kristy in the months leading up to the wedding, one could see an evident *agape* love. On their wedding day, Kristy was beautiful, yet very frail. Her first dance with Sam was a testimony of love: because she could hardly stand, Sam held her tightly, practically carrying her through the dance. Their newlywed bliss was, sadly, cut short. Kristy died within two weeks of the wedding.

Sam showed us all what *agape* love was: unconditional, sacrificial.

"Love binds the bridegroom (husband) to be concerned for the good of the bride (wife)" (*TOB* 92:4). *Agape* love wills, above all else, the good of the other person. When love is no longer focused on personal gratification or comfort, but lays down one's life and pleasure for what the other person needs, *agape* love is blooming.

But our *eros* is not destroyed by *agape* love. It would be inaccurate to pit one love against another, as if they were opposed. When *eros* is freed of selfishness, it is caught up in and transformed by *agape*. Without ceasing to exist, our desire (*eros*) for our spouse is unified with a generous and sacrificial love (*agape*).

We love seeing *agape* love in romantic films or certain superhero films where the hero risks his or her life for a loved one or someone else. But *agape* love is often lived much more quietly: in embracing daily household chores, being kind and patient when a loved one is suffering, forgiving when we have been wronged and letting go of our hurt, putting the needs of our spouse or child before our own.

Our God is no stranger to this *agape* love, for "God's *eros* for man is also totally *agape*," Pope Benedict XVI wrote.[6] God's plan from the beginning was to show and call us to this pinnacle of love, and he used a vehicle common to us all to show us this great love: the human body.

---

6. Ibid., no. 10.

Daily Challenge

Share a time when your spouse showed you agape love. Ask your spouse one way you can serve him or her, putting your spouse before yourself, this week. Maybe a foot massage, helping with the dishes, a love note, a date night, or a slow dance to your wedding song, etc. Make it concrete and write it down, if need be.

Prayer

Lord, help us to be more like you. Help us to be less selfish and more giving. Help us to see the good in each other, even as we get to know one another's idiosyncrasies and failings. Purify our desires with your *agape* love, so we may glorify you in our bodies and love you with all our hearts, all our souls, all our minds, and all our strength (see Mk 12:30).

✑

DAY FIVE

Loving Our Spouse "Incarnationally"

> Through the fact that the Word of God became flesh the body entered theology . . . through the main door. (*TOB* 23:4)

The incarnation is God's great love story for us! It is the moment when love became visible, taking on a human body. Pondering the great mystery of our God who became man should be our focus every Christmas season.

In all the busyness of Christmas shopping, Black Friday deals, stringing up lights, wearing ugly sweaters, and preparing for drama with relatives, we can forget this essential point of Christmas: God entered the world as a human being to free us from sin and bring us back to himself.

> For God so loved the world that he gave his only Son, so that everyone who believes in him might not perish but might have eternal life. (Jn 3:16)

The word "incarnation" comes from the Latin "*caro,*" meaning "flesh," so the meaning is literally "to be made into flesh." God used the material of his beloved creation—the human body—to become visible and to show us how to love with the fullness of all the loves we've been examining: *storge*, *philia*, *eros*, and *agape*.

Christ grew in obedience to his parents, Mary and Joseph. He worked with his hands, learned his faith, cultivated friendships, and eventually embarked on his greatest mission of self-sacrifice. Jesus experienced all aspects of life *through* his body: hunger and thirst, joy and pain, comfort and suffering. No doubt he felt *storge* love for his family and *philia* love for his apostles. The *eros* of Christ led him to seek his Father in the intimacy of his prayers, and his *agape* love led him to the Cross.

Jesus' body was essential to God's plan, for "the flesh is the hinge of salvation" (*CCC* 1015). *Our* bodies are essential as well. We're not disembodied spirits or spiritual beings trapped in the prison of a body. *We are our bodies*—we are a unique combination of body and soul, and we cannot experience life in any other form. Through his death and resurrection, Jesus has redeemed and taken the human body up to a position of glory and he calls all of us to the same glorious transformation.

> Only when Christ is formed in us will the mystery of Christmas be fulfilled in us. Christmas is the mystery of this marvelous exchange: "O marvelous exchange! Man's Creator has become man, born of the Virgin. We have been made sharers in the divinity of Christ who humbled himself to share in our humanity." (*CCC* 526)

By allowing Christ to be made incarnate in us—through prayer and the sacraments, especially the Eucharist—we learn to live love in all its forms. We learn to love our spouse "incarnationally," which means that we love as Christ would love. We become the hands and feet of Christ in our marriage, loving and serving one another.

Daily Challenge

Since beginning this devotional, how has your view of the body changed? Has your view of Jesus changed? Imagine yourself at the nativity scene. Picture yourself holding Baby Jesus in your arms: What does he look like? What does he smell like? What sounds is he making?

Prayer

Read verses two and three of "Hark, the Herald Angels Sing." (You don't have to sing, but feel free!)

Christ, by highest heaven adored;
Christ, the everlasting Lord;
late in time behold him come,
offspring of a virgin's womb.
Veiled in flesh the Godhead see;
hail th' incarnate Deity,
pleased with us in flesh to dwell,
Jesus, our Emmanuel.
Hark! the herald angels sing,
"Glory to the new born King!"
Hail the heaven-born Prince of Peace!
Hail the Sun of Righteousness!
Light and life to all he brings,
risen with healing in his wings.
Mild he lays his glory by,
born that we no more may die,
born to raise us from the earth,
born to give us second birth.
Hark! the herald angels sing,
"Glory to the new born King!"

༄

Day Six

The Scandal of the Cross

If you were raised Catholic, you have probably been staring at crucifixes your entire life, whether in a classroom, above a door in your house, or at every Mass your parents ever dragged you to. The depiction of a man nailed to a Cross may have become almost commonplace to you. When we grow up close to something so profound, we risk taking it for granted. We can forget how much of a scandal the Cross was and is. And even worse, we can forget that we're looking at an image of God's love.

If the Cross could be considered the "logo" or "brand" of our faith, we sure seem to have picked a depressing one!

Beaten and bloody, this God-man named Jesus embraced every misunderstanding, hurt, and sin of the world and allowed himself to be nailed to a Cross. He experienced lashing and intense pain. He struggled to breathe. In fact, the word "excruciating" used to describe terrible pain is derived from the Latin, *ex* "out of," and *cruciare*, "to crucify."

You might ask yourself, "Why is crucifixion the climax of God's great love story? If God is really love, why such a violent and gruesome ending?" The crucifixion of our Lord makes absolutely no sense if we view love as a mere feeling. If love is simply what "feels good," then Jesus could have been hugged to death or shot with fluffy bunnies. Our God, who could have chosen any way to die, chose to die a painful and agonizing death.

Why?

It is part of the nature of life-giving love (*agape*) that it is sacrificial. Love demands real expense, not warm, fuzzy feelings. Saint Teresa of Kolkata said that for love to be real, it must require sacrifice, it must hurt. The examples of sacrificial love in the world almost always bring some suffering and pain. Any woman who has been in labor knows that all the pain is worth it when she *finally* sees the amazing child who had been forming in her womb for months. Ecstasy follows agony, but the agony must first be embraced.

In a similar way, Scripture says that it was "for the sake of the joy that lay before [Jesus] that he endured the cross" (Heb 12:2b). What was that joy? Jesus endured the pain of the Cross and bore the weight of our sin on his shoulders so that we could live in freedom from sin and spend all eternity with our God of love in heaven (see Gal 5:1).

Now *that* is GOOD NEWS! Christianity is not about being "nice" to one another, but about celebrating God, who became man, and following his example of self-emptying love.

For those who are called to the married vocation, Jesus is our model of love. He shows us how to love our beloved. Jesus, the Divine Bridegroom, laid down his life for the Church, the Bride. The crucifixion is God's proposal to us. On the Cross, God is saying, "I give everything for love of you. I lay down my life for you. Will you give me all of you in return?"

Not only does God want to wed us to himself for all eternity, but he also shows each bride and bridegroom what love really looks like. In each marriage, the bride and bridegroom can look to the Cross for inspiration to love in a complete and sacrificial way.

Daily Challenge

Find a crucifix in your home or a photo of one on the Internet and place it between you and your spouse. As you gaze on the crucifix, pray the Sorrowful Mysteries of the Rosary together and end with the prayer below.

Prayer

When I survey the wondrous Cross
on which the Prince of Glory died,
my richest gain, I count but loss,
and pour contempt on all my pride.
See from his head, his hands, his feet,
sorrow and love flow mingled down!
Did ever such love and sorrow meet,
or thorns compose so rich a crown!
Were the whole realm of nature mine,
that were an offering far too small;
love so amazing, so divine,
demands my soul, my life, my all.[7]

---

7. Isaac Watts, "The Wonderful Cross," from *The Psalms and Hymns of Isaac Watts* (London: C. Whittingham, 1806), hymn no. 7.

✌

DAY SEVEN

Jesus the Bridegroom

Saint Teresa of Kolkata devoted her life to serving the poor and outcast of India. She credited any effectiveness in her ministry to the power of Christ, particularly in the Eucharist. She would say that we can look at the crucifix to understand how much Jesus loves us, and we can look at the Eucharist to understand how much he loves us in the here and now.

We have seen how the bodily suffering of Christ on the Cross is our model of *agape* love lived to its extreme. This is the bar set by God himself, and it also beckons us to love in this same way. In the upcoming weeks, we will look at how the Church asks us to live out this *agape* love, especially within the context of marriage. But the food for this life-long journey of faith is Christ himself in "the source and summit of the Christian life" (*CCC* 1324): the Eucharist.

More than a mere sign or symbol, we believe that Jesus is *truly present* in the consecrated host. It is a great mystery, but this is at the core of our faith. If you've gone through the motions at Mass for your entire life, pay close attention the next time you go. As the priest prays over the humble bread and wine, ask for the gift of faith to see what takes place at a deeper level as the bread and wine become Jesus' Body and Blood.

The Mass is a re-presentation of Christ's sacrifice on the Cross—the Body of the Groom laid down for his Bride. We are united to Christ and his body as we literally *consume his Body* and take it into ourselves. No, we're not cannibals (although the early Christians were no strangers to this accusation). But we can all acknowledge that there is *something* within us that desires to consume or be one with those we love. Sometimes we hear or say, "I could just eat up" an adorable baby. You share a kiss with your beloved is an attempt (at some level) to be one with the other person. The closest we can get to our spouse here on this earth is to become "one flesh" with them in the act of intercourse, a deeply personal act of communion.

As Pope Benedict XVI expressed, the Eucharist—also called Holy Communion—"corresponds to the union of man and woman in marriage. Just as they become 'one flesh,' so in Communion, we all become 'one spirit,' one person, with Christ."[8]

That's right: Marriage and the Eucharist are intimately tied together.

The act of communion with your spouse is a big deal because we are made in the very image and likeness of God who is a communion of persons: Father, Son, and Holy Spirit. God has left us the Eucharist, a sacred communion, as spiritual nourishment. Truly, no man is an island; we are made for and desire communion.

Next time you are at Mass, when you hear the words, "The Body of Christ," remember that these are the words of the Divine Bridegroom who desires union with you, his beloved spouse. As you walk in the Communion line, realize that you are actually

---

8. Benedict XVI, *Spirit of the Liturgy* (San Francisco: Ignatius Press, 2000), 142.

"walking down the aisle" toward Jesus the Bridegroom. And every time you say, "Amen," remember that you are saying, "I do" to the One who gives his Body up for you in order to be in union with you.

Next week we will look more deeply into this mystery of love and explore the role marriage plays in God's plan of love.

Daily Challenge

Pick out a day in the coming week to go to daily Mass with your spouse. Masses may be available in your area in the early morning or in the evening. If your schedule doesn't allow for a daily Mass, make a date with your spouse to go to your local Catholic Church and pray in front of the Blessed Sacrament (whether exposed in a monstrance or in the tabernacle). If you have the time, make an entire Holy Hour of Adoration before the Blessed Sacrament.

Prayer

Soul of Christ, sanctify me.
Body of Christ, save me.
Blood of Christ, cleanse me.
Water from the side of Christ, wash me.
Passion of Christ, strengthen me.
Good Jesus, hear me.
Within your wounds hide me.
Never let me be parted from you.
From the evil one protect me.

In the hour of my death, call me
and bid me come to you,
that with your saints I may praise you
forever and ever. Amen.

WEEK THREE

What Is Marriage?

Day One

Written in Our Bodies

We all love weddings. The bride and the groom, the pomp and circumstance, the flowers and festivities, the party and dancing—everything about weddings seems to excite and call out of us a desire to recognize a loving union. Weddings are celebrated around the world, some humbly and others quite elaborately. Many great films or television shows seems to either incorporate or end with a wedding.

Why is that? Why do weddings brings us such delight and joy?

Marriage and the call to the wedding feast is a reality *written into our very bodies*: "'God himself is the author of marriage.' The vocation to marriage is written in the very nature of man and woman as they came from the hand of the Creator" (*CCC* 1603).

In Scripture, God's love for the Chosen People of Israel is constantly sprinkled with the language of bride and groom, and when Israel turns away from God, the language reflects that of a betrayed lover. As we noted before, the Bible itself, God's own

Word, begins and ends with a wedding—the first wedding of male and female, Adam and Eve, and the final wedding in heaven between Christ and the Church.

Marriage is at the *center* of our Christian story. God saw fit to make it the earthly vehicle for his great message of love, and rather than a mere contractual union, he elevated marriage to a sacrament.

You may remember your seventh grade definition of a "sacrament" as something like, "a visible sign instituted by Christ of an invisible grace." In other words, a sacrament is a mystery of divine reality visible to us by a physical sign.

Sacraments need visible symbols because we are visible, concrete beings and cannot experience life any other way. What's more, for the sacrament to be effective, the precise matter is important. You cannot have the Eucharist with a doughnut and coffee; you need unleavened bread and wine. You cannot have Baptism with vinegar and peanut oil; you need water and the sacred chrism oil. The concrete signs of the male and female bodies are the essential matter for the sacrament of Marriage. All sacraments need the necessary sign or their meaning is obscured or outright lost.

Saint John Paul II calls marriage the "primordial" (or first) sacrament of God's love, as well as the "sacrament of redemption." Wow! That's no small honor. But how is marriage the "first" sacrament as well as the sacrament of our redemption? We will examine Saint Paul's letter to the Ephesians tomorrow to find the answer. We will also look at a controversial passage referred to as the "crowning" text by John Paul II in *Man and Woman He Created Them: A Theology of the Body*.

Daily Challenge

What was the best wedding (besides your own if you are married) you've ever been to? What made it so special? If you are married, share what you remember most about your wedding day. What were the highlights and what were some crazy moments? If you are not married yet, discuss your ideal wedding.

Prayer

Lord, thank you for the gift of marriage. Thank you for being the Author of marriage and for bringing the two of us together. Marriage is a call to be the sign of your love to the world. Give us the grace to either discern if this is your will for our relationship or to continue to be that sign of love every day.

꩜

Day Two

The Marks of Authentic Love

Be subject to one another out of reverence for Christ. Wives, be subject to your husbands as you are to the Lord. For the husband is the head of the wife just as Christ is the head of the church, the body of which he is the Savior. Just as the church is subject to Christ, so also wives ought to be, in everything, to their husbands.

Husbands, love your wives, just as Christ loved the church and gave himself up for her, in order to make her holy by cleansing her with the washing of water by the word, so as to present the church to himself in splendor, without a spot or wrinkle or anything of the kind—yes, so that she may be holy and without blemish. In the same way, husbands should love their wives as they do their own bodies. He who loves his wife loves himself. For no one ever hates his own body, but he nourishes and tenderly cares for it, just as Christ does for the church, because we are members of his body. "For this reason a man will leave his father and mother and be joined to his wife, and the two will become one flesh." This is a great mystery, and I am applying it to Christ and the church. Each of you, however, should love his wife as himself, and a wife should respect her husband. (Eph 5:21–33)

We know some brave couples who have had the above passage from Saint Paul's letter to the Ephesians read at their weddings. These couples were not bothered by the command, "Wives be subject to your husbands" (or "*subordinate* to," or "*submissive* to," depending on the translation). They were undisturbed because they understood and embraced the reality that is at the heart of Paul's words in this passage.

Many miss it, but the central command here is for husbands to love their wives in an utterly sacrificial way—as Christ loved the Church. Just as Christ sacrificed his life for his Bride, the Church, husbands are called to help their wives get to heaven ("to *sanctify* her"). And if wives are to be in submission to this, what that really means is that a wife is "under the mission" ("submission") of the husband. The wife submits then to this beautiful mission of her husband who is called to lay down his life for her.

Christ came to serve, not to be served, and this is the model he sets for every person embarking on the journey of love. Every husband ought to be a servant leader who is willing to "wash the feet" of his bride every night. (Not literally, unless your wife has really stinky feet!) This passage then is really a call to *mutual submission* between both spouses, a truly selfless dynamic of love between a husband and wife. As Saint John Paul II writes, to submit to one's spouse means to be "completely given" as a true reciprocal gift of self (*TOB* 90:2).

The mutual submission of love meant to occur between spouses is intrinsically connected to the bodily language of reciprocal gift. As we saw last week, the language of both Christ on the Cross and in the Eucharist is the language of self-gift. Indeed, "bodily love" is meant to express the "language of agape," which is sacrificial and embraces the crosses of life whenever they arise (*TOB* 92:7). John Paul II wrote that, "it is the body itself that 'speaks'; it speaks with its masculinity or femininity, it speaks with the mysterious language of the personal gift" (*TOB* 104:4).

Without words, our own bodies speak a very real language. It's easy to tell when our loved one is angry or frustrated because we can (hopefully) pick up signals through their body language or lack of communication. We likewise can show affection for a person by how we rest on their shoulder or cry in their arms. We possess the ability to speak real love through our bodies, and this is a great responsibility.

To be considered authentic love, as defined by our Catholic faith, there are four characteristic marks for this language of the body: *free*, *total*, *faithful*, and *fruitful*. These four marks can be used as a litmus test to determine whether our love meets the sacrificial, *agape* demands of authentic marital love.

These four marks are also embedded within the promises and the vows we make on our wedding day. To love freely, totally, faithfully, and fruitfully is to truly love in accordance with the language of our bodies and the great mystery of how Christ loved us all. We will examine these marks of love in the coming days.

Daily Challenge

Open your own Bible and read aloud (again) the passage from Ephesians 5:21–33. What do you feel when you read this passage? What line sticks out to you the most? What word or words challenge or strike you? Why? Share these insights with your spouse.

Prayer

Jesus, you are the model of love and you show us how to lay down our lives out of reverence for each other. Help us to love each other as you have loved us.

Day Three

Free—Loving Without Reservation

For freedom Christ set us free, therefore do not submit again to the yoke of slavery. (Gal 5:1)

Many magazines and online articles boast headlines such as: "124 Ways to Make Him (or Her) Fall in Love With You." These kinds of headlines ought to elicit a chuckle because, besides being obvious click bait, coercing a person to love you ought to sound ridiculous to just about anyone.

As we know from movies or TV shows containing genies or magic spells, there seems to a rule that it's impossible to make someone love another person. No matter what the protagonist wishes, love is a cosmic power too great to be tamed or controlled because it can only be received freely. A profound truth is revealed here.

Love can never be forced. To be love, love must be free. In your best Scottish accent, "Freedom!" is the first of our four marks of authentic love. Freedom exists not merely for the sake of freedom but *for* the sake of love. To be free for the sake of marriage means that no one—spouse, mother, father-in-law, priest, or friend—can force you to vow your love to another person in either a shotgun wedding or an arranged marriage. A marriage also must be free from other impediments that would invalidate it (for example if a spouse plans not to be faithful).

The importance of this mark of love is evident in the wedding ceremony when the couple is asked if they have come together freely to be married.

In promising your freedom, you're saying that you're not attached to anyone else (whether lawfully, emotionally, or physically). You're also promising to avoid enslavement to any*thing* else, whether alcohol, pornography, or any other addiction. Authentic love strives for freedom *from* unhealthy relationships and enslavement to sin in order to be free *for* virtue and life-giving relationships. Saint John Paul II writes: "Indeed, inasmuch as he is master over himself he can 'give himself' to another" (*TOB* 123:5). In other words, if we can't say "no," then our "yes" is incomplete.

The Church does not set arbitrary standards to make our love lives more complicated. These are the marks of love because we are made in the image of God and *this is how God loves.* Any love that is not free (or total, faithful, or fruitful) will not satisfy our hearts; such a love is a mere counterfeit.

These four marks are also how God showed his love from the Cross. Christ laid down his life freely. Nobody forced him to do it. Despite the mockery, the misunderstanding, the beating, and the suffering he endured, he willingly embraced his Cross.

> I lay down my life in order to take it up again. No one takes it from me, but I lay it down of my own accord. I have power to lay it down, and I have power to take it up again. I have received this command from my Father. (Jn 10:14–18)

Real *agape* love leads to a natural willingness to freely offer one's life for the sake of her or his spouse.

Daily Challenge

Do you have any attachments or sins you wish to be free from in order to love your spouse more perfectly (e.g., pride, lust, pornography, envy, laziness, gluttony, etc.)? Be specific, and even though it may be a difficult or sensitive subject, share your reflections with one another. Find some time this week to go on a date night and, if possible, begin the night with the sacrament of Confession at a local parish.

Prayer

Thank you, Jesus, for freely giving yourself to us that we might be free. Heal our bodies, minds, hearts, and souls of any unhealthy attachments so that we might be truly free to love God, our neighbor, and ourselves.

༄

Day Four

Total—Body, Heart, Mind, and Soul

From Jackie: I knew that Bobby was the man I was called to marry when I realized that, for the first time, I could finally be myself in a relationship. I didn't have to pretend to be someone I was not, and I didn't have to hide parts of my personality for fear he would break up with me. The parts of me that scared other guys off—whether it was that I go to daily Mass and love the Rosary and Adoration and spiritual books OR that I'm a total goofball and at times crazy and loud and have a weird sense of humor—strangely attracted Bobby even more. In past relationships, guys were attracted to some parts of me and not to others, but with Bobby I knew that he loved *all* of me—body, soul, heart, and mind.

And that love was mutual. For the first time in my life, the more I knew about Bobby and the more I spent time with him, the more I loved all of him, even in the midst of arguments, even through the sufferings and circumstances of life, and even after seeing his quirks and failings. With other men, the more I got to know them, the more I was disappointed or hurt. With Bobby, the more I truly knew him, the more deeply I respected and cared for him.

We all desire to be loved completely and totally. We don't want to be loved only for what we can give, whether that's pleasure, status, or security. When someone only stays with us when we are successful or good-looking or feeling good, then we feel like objects of use. We also don't want someone just to love the idea of us, yet dread actually being with us in the messiness of our humanity. Every human heart desires to be loved when we are at our best *and* our worst, in all our strengths and weaknesses, in all our oddities and foibles. We don't want to be loved just for our bodies, but also our minds, our hearts, and our souls.

In fact, the *Catechism of the Catholic Church* affirms this truth, when it says:

> Conjugal love involves a totality in which all the elements of the person enter—appeal of the body and instinct, power of feeling and affectivity, aspiration of the spirit and of will. It aims at a deeply personal unity, a unity that, beyond union in one flesh, leads to forming one heart and soul. (1643)

We are called to love and be loved totally because Christ loved us this way, and we only know how to love "because he first loved us" (1 Jn 4:19). On the Cross, Jesus held nothing back. He gave us every part of himself: body, blood, soul, and divinity. He also loved *us* totally.

As Saint Paul wrote: "God proves his love for us in that while we still were sinners Christ died for us" (Rom 5:8). God didn't just die for the righteous, or those who have great marriages and families, or those who seem to have it all together. No, he also died for the broken, addicted, disobedient, lazy, gluttonous, murderous, prideful, and lustful.

Isn't that all of us, though? God loves us not only when we are sinless and triumphant in virtue, but also when we act like whiny, tantrum-throwing brats and wallow in the muck of vice. His is a love that loves *totally*.

Daily Challenge

Share with your spouse four of your favorite things about him or her (one from each: body, mind, heart, and soul).

Prayer

God, thank you for loving us even when we turn from you, even when we are not faithful, even when we forget you. Thank you for showing us how to love totally, and may we love one another in all the good and bad, our gifts and weaknesses, our virtues and brokenness.

DAY FIVE

Faithful—Until Death Do Us Part

From Bobby: Before our wedding, Jackie told me this cool story about a village in Bosnia Herzegovina that has a zero percent divorce rate. We did some research and discovered that every couple who is married there makes their vows while holding a crucifix. Then they kiss the Cross. That crucifix is a daily reminder that their love must walk the way of Jesus on the Cross—their marriage must be free, total, faithful, and fruitful.

On our wedding day, using a crucifix that Jackie brought back from the Holy Land, we said our vows in a similar way. We held the crucifix in our hands as we made our vows, then we kissed the feet of Jesus on the Cross. That crucifix is now hanging over our bed as a daily reminder that our marriage must model the selfless agape love of Christ.

Trust me, I need all the reminders I can get of that great call: "Husbands, love your wives, just as Christ loved the church" (Eph 5:25). When toddlers are crying, when I'm tired or grumpy, or when I just want my way on any given issue, that crucifix literally hangs over my head to bring me back to my vows and promises. It's a constant reminder that God has given us the sacrament of Marriage as means for our sanctification—marriage, if embraced joyfully, will make us holy.

We need holy husbands and wives just as much as we need holy priests, brothers, and sisters. Holiness is not the call of a special, privileged few. Christ wants all of us to love in a life-giving, transformative way.

Righteous anger is a natural human response to infidelity. For every love song on the radio that pledges lifelong fidelity, describes warm bubbly feelings, and praises unconditional love, there is a song of lament heartbreak, betrayal, and vengeance (often involving property destruction).

Of the four marks we are examining, the modern world seems to most clearly understand the importance of being *faithful* (although it does not always value it in practice). Even without the language of theology or religion, we all know at some level that we are not meant to be used, abused, betrayed, or cheated on.

The Latin word *fides* is a root word for "fidelity" and "infidelity," and *fides* means faith. We are made for faithful love, and deep down we can sense this. Yet in our fallen world, the airwaves are flooded with shows glorifying promiscuous bachelors and bachelorettes, broken marriages, cheating spouses, and men and women sleeping around without consequence. Commitment is not always esteemed in our media and entertainment, but we all ache for faithful love because we were made in the image of God, who is faithful.

The following Scripture passages describe the nature of God's faithfulness:

> Know therefore that the Lord your God is God, the faithful God who maintains covenant loyalty with those who love

him and keep his commandments, to a thousand generations. (Deut 7:9)

God is faithful; by him you were called into the fellowship of his Son, Jesus Christ our Lord. (1 Cor 1:9)

Can a woman forget her nursing child,
or show no compassion for the child of her womb?
Even these may forget,
yet I will not forget you. (Is 49:15)

If my father and mother forsake me,
the Lord will take me up. (Ps 27:10)

God's faithful love is *unconditional*. Even when we betray or abandon God, he will never leave or forsake us. When we make our vows on our wedding day, we *also* promise to love unconditionally. It would be silly to say, "I promise to love you until you get fat, old, and ugly—and then I'm going to find someone skinnier, younger, and better looking. I promise to love you until you mess up—then I'm going to find someone who never frustrates me." Rather, we promise to honor one another until "death do us part."

Jesus reminds us that in the life to come we will no longer have need for marriage (see Mt 22:30). But we *will* know and love and be able to "see" our spouse in a deeper and more profound way than we ever did here on earth. In that eternal banquet we will enter into the love that lasts forever, but on this side of the heavenly veil we make our pledge until parted by death.

We promise fidelity not only in the "big moments" of marriage, but also in the little moments of daily life. In the daily grind of work, home life, raising children, and recreation, am I being attentive to my spouse? Am I recognizing the needs of the other person? Am I only focused on my own pleasure and desires? Do I allow little frustrations and annoyances to rob me of the joy of being with the person I love? We begin to live heroic, sacrificial love in the little moments of everyday life. Loving one day at a time leads to a lifetime of love.

While a lifetime may seem to us like a long time to be faithful to one person, God promises to love us for *all eternity*. Let us honor our spouses for as long as we live on this earth and rejoice that we have a faithful God who will love us forever.

Daily Challenge

When you were growing up, what were some examples of faithfulness for you? Did you have models of unfaithfulness? How did these examples influence your relationships? Discuss these points with your spouse.

Prayer

Lord, thank you for your faithful love. Help us to be faithful to you and to one another, in big and small ways, all the days of our lives.

◈

Day Six

Fruitful—"Be Fruitful and Multiply"

The Hebrew Bible (the "Old Testament" for Christians), contains 613 commandments referred to as "Mosaic Law." The very first commandment, however, is found in Genesis 1:28 when God blesses Adam and Eve and says, "Be fruitful and multiply."

No, God was not telling Adam and Eve to distribute apples and oranges while practicing their multiplication tables. He was telling them to become "one flesh" and make babies! God is not only telling us that sex is good, but also that its natural, biological end—the fruitfulness of children—is also good.

Fruitfulness is the fourth mark of authentic love that we promise on our wedding day before God and his people. Saint John Paul II explains that when a couple speaks the truth of the language of the body, then the "conjugal act 'means' not only love, but also potential fruitfulness" (*TOB* 123:6). Thus, in the marriage vows, when a couple is asked if they will accept children from God, the man and woman answer, "Yes."

The language of love is fruitful because the nature of love is creative and diffusive—love *wants* to go out of itself and create. That's why God, who is Love, chose to create the world; it's part of his nature to want to diffuse his love. And it's pretty amazing that God allows us, his creatures, to share in the act of creation. We participate in and witness a child being "knit" in his mother's womb (see Ps 139:13).

When a couple promises to be fruitful within their marriage, they promise not only to be open to physical fruitfulness (or children), but also to spiritual fruitfulness. That's why couples who are physically unable bear children can still be *spiritually* fruitful in their marriage. Couples who are unable to have children often have many spiritual children (whether as godparents or as mentors in ministry or teaching). And their witness of marriage can show the world the fruits of the Holy Spirit: peace, patience, charity, kindness, faithfulness generosity, gentleness, goodness, self-control, modesty, chastity, and joy.

Scripture says that you will know a tree by its fruit (see Mt 7:17). By this standard, couples will be able to know whether they are living their vow of "fruitfulness" in marriage by the fruits of the Spirit that come forth from their union. Others will recognize married Christians by their openness to children (even when it is not possible) as well as their love, peace, and joy.

As always, our model of fruitfulness is Jesus Christ himself. When Christ, the Bridegroom, laid down his life on the Cross for his Bride, the Church, it was so that we may go and "bear fruit, fruit that will last" (Jn 15:16). Let us also ask Our Lady, the Blessed Virgin Mary, to pray for us to be fruitful in our marriages, since Christ was literally the "fruit of her womb." May we, too, bear Christ and bring him into the world.

Daily Challenge

Of the fruits of the Holy Spirit listed above, which do you see most in your relationship with your spouse? Share your thoughts with one another.

Prayer

Holy Spirit, enlighten our minds, inflame our souls, and purify our hearts so that we may bear the fruits of the Spirit in our lives and in our marriage. May people who encounter us encounter you. May our marriage be a witness of God's love.

❧

Day Seven

The Words Made Flesh

Couples often have different reminders of their marriage around the house. Sometimes it is a crucifix, a wedding picture, or a special gift they received. These objects are reminders of their vows and that special day. And yet, the vows are not yet *complete* until they became incarnate and the "two became one flesh."

What does that mean in clear and simple language?

It means that every time a couple has sex, they are renewing their wedding vows! The words "free, total, faithful, and fruitful" that are used in the vows are the same language our bodies speak when we become one flesh with our spouse. In the marital embrace, our bodies are saying, "I will love you freely, totally, faithfully, and fruitfully." This is the truth of our bodies! This is the language of the body!

Saint John Paul II explains it like this:

> [W]ithout this consummation, marriage is not yet constituted in its full reality. . . . In fact, the words themselves, "I take you as my wife/as my husband" . . . can only be fulfilled by . . . conjugal intercourse. (*TOB* 103:2)

In his "Letter to Families" *(Gratissimam Sane)*:

> All married life is a gift; but this becomes most evident when the spouses, in giving themselves to each other in

love, bring about that encounter which makes them "one flesh."[1]

If our bodies can speak a truth, they can also speak a *lie*. When bodies unite in the act of sex, they are promising to be total gift for one another, something that the lips of the couple may never have said. For this reason, John Paul II considered sex outside of marriage as an act of "lying with our bodies," since bodies are speaking the language of a promise that was never made. This is one of the Church's main issues with premarital sex, or any sexual act outside the bonds of marriage—the body is making promises without any commitment to a vowed, lifelong union.

In "On Love in the Family" (*Amoris Laetitia*), Pope Francis wrote that, "Sexuality is not a means of gratification or entertainment; it is an interpersonal language wherein the other is taken seriously, in his or her sacred and inviolable dignity."[2] Whereas the modern world treats sex as entertainment, the Church calls us to *fully* receive the gift of human sexuality in all its beauty and magnitude.

Let us be sure to recognize this great responsibility to live and speak the truth of the body with love and joy, so that our

---

1. John Paul II, *Gratissimam Sane*, Vatican Web site, February 2, 1994, no. 12, accessed Nov. 3, 2016, http://w2.vatican.va/content/john-paul-ii/en/letters/1994/documents/hf_jp-ii_let_02021994_families.html.

2. Francis, *Amoris Laetitia*, Vatican Web site, March 19, 2016, no. 151, http://w2.vatican.va/content/francesco/en/apost_exhortations/documents/papa-francesco_esortazione-ap_20160319_amoris-laetitia.html.

marriage may be a living sign of a free, total, faithful, and fruitful love.

Daily Challenge

Now, if you are married, go renew and incarnate your wedding vows (we won't tell anybody). If you aren't married, offer up a prayer together asking for the courage to wait until marriage and to resist all temptation.

Prayer

Lord, help us to love one another freely, totally, faithfully, and fruitfully. As we look forward to or remember our wedding vows, may we remember to love as you loved and to lay down our lives as gift for one another.

WEEK FOUR

How Can Our Love Last?

Day One

The One Who Satisfies

To love freely, totally, faithfully, and fruitfully is a great call, and we should feel blessed if God has called us to marriage with an amazing spouse. But we risk making marriage into an idol if we imagine marriage satisfies our every hope and dream.

The ache you feel in your soul—that longing you feel for completion, a longing that emerged first in the original solitude of Adam—doesn't go away in marriage. If anything, that ache *deepens* when we realize that our spouse can *never* satisfy the infinite ache of our souls.

> The desire for God is written in the human heart, because man is created by God and for God; and God never ceases to draw man to himself. Only in God will he find the truth and happiness he never stops searching for: The dignity of man rests above all on the fact that he is called to communion with God. (*CCC* 27)

The sooner we realize and accept that Christ alone will fill our restless hearts, the sooner we can have a marriage that truly satisfies.

Jackie: The happiest day of my life was not my wedding day. Some people may gasp at that sentiment, since the day we get married is when life really begins, when we can finally be blissfully happy, and when all of our aches and longings for love are finally quenched, right?

If you're married, you're probably already chuckling. Maybe that's what you thought when you were single: that marriage would solve all your problems, fix your brokenness, and satisfy every bit of your loneliness.

Well, thankfully I can say, that God crushed those notions for me before I got married. Why? Because my wedding day was only the second happiest day of my life. The first was when I gave myself fully to someone other than my husband: God.

At the age of eighteen, my world was turned upside down at a youth conference. There, I realized that the God who loved me so much that he gave everything for me on the Cross desired that I give him my whole life in return, not just one hour on Sunday. I realized that God wanted all of me: my gifts, weaknesses, relationships, vocation, job, time, talent, and treasure. He proposed his divine love story to me and I said, "Yes."

For ten years before I met Bobby, God wooed me, and I fell more and more in love with him. I saw Jesus every day at Mass, I got to know him more deeply through Scripture, and I went on dates with him in Adoration. I even got to know his mom, Mary, pretty well, and I began to love her dearly.

During this time, I learned something that has been extremely helpful in marriage: God is the ultimate Bridegroom—

the one for whom I was made to spend all eternity with in heaven. He alone can fix my brokenness and satisfy every ache and longing in my heart. He alone is perfect.

While my husband is my best friend, the love of my life, and the man of my dreams, I know that he is not God. He has weaknesses and foibles, and sometimes he loves imperfectly. I am glad he also knows that God alone satisfies his heart and that God is first in our marriage, because this means he also realizes that I am not perfect and do not love perfectly.

Whew, that definitely takes pressure off of a relationship! It allows us to be human and to avoid putting one another on a pedestal (one from which we are sure to fall). When we put God first and our spouse second, we are able to love our spouse more fully. Thus, in order to love our spouse better, we must love God better, since he shows us how to love others rightly.

On our wedding day, it was beautiful when Bobby and I, side by side and hand in hand, faced the crucifix and the altar. I realized that we were both standing before the Bridegroom of our souls, Jesus Christ, and that was the primary relationship from which our love for one another found its source.

Daily Challenge

Examine how you viewed marriage growing up. Did you ever plan your wedding as a small child or teenager? What was important to you then? Have you ever made marriage into an idol? Discuss this with your spouse.

Prayer

"You have formed us for yourself, and our hearts are restless till they find rest in you."[1]

---

1. Augustine, *Confessions*, in *Nicene and Post-Nicene Fathers, First Series*, vol. 1, ed. Philip Schaff, trans. J. G. Pilkington (Buffalo, NY: Christian Literature Publishing Co., 1887), rev. and ed. for New Advent by Kevin Knight, bk. 1, chap. 1. http://www.newadvent.org/fathers/110101.htm.

ॐ

DAY TWO

God Cares Who You Marry

God is a loving communion of persons who desires that we *incarnate* his love here on earth. That's a serious task! So it goes without saying that if you are called to marriage, you should probably pick the right traveling buddy for this journey of life-giving love.

We can be tempted, however, by two extreme viewpoints when discerning the right spouse. One extreme is that of the idealized "soul mate." This is the idea that God has preordained the perfect person for you and you both will ride off on a unicorn into the sunset, perfectly happy forever after. All you have to do, apparently, is sit around and wait until this person crashes into your living room.

The other extreme insists that you will always marry the wrong person. Basically, this is the idea that there is no perfect person for you. God doesn't really care. You would be equally happy (or miserable) with about forty different people. So just pick one and get on with your life.

There's been no official document from the Church on "soul mates" but since most virtue is in the middle of two extremes, it seems fair to guess that the virtuous perspective probably lies in the middle here as well.

Marriage "in its deepest essence, *emerges from the mystery* of God's eternal love for . . . humanity" (*TOB* 90:4). Pope Francis writes: "The sacrament of marriage is not a social convention, an empty ritual, or merely the outward sign of a commitment. The sacrament is a gift given for the sanctification and salvation of the spouses."[2]

In other words, God *cares* who you marry. You were fashioned by him before time existed—every hair on your head has been counted! If he indeed has plans for your welfare and not your woe (see Jer 29:11), he probably has a person in mind for you to marry. This is no trivial matter to him.

Our job then is to trust that God will provide and to wait on his timing. If we trust God, we avoid settling for any person who breathes or grasping for the wrong kind of love out of fear. Settling out of fear and grasping for love outside of God's time were the fundamental sins of Adam and Eve.

No matter what, your spouse will be flawed because we are all human beings. We can't be so picky that we're only focused on the superficial elements of a person (e.g., he must be a doctor or she must be a supermodel). But we also shouldn't settle for someone just because he or she is the comfortable or safe option. God does not want you to be miserable. You ought to *desire* your spouse and they ought to *desire* what is best for you and want you to go to heaven.

Is there a real friendship beneath your romance?

Can you pray with your spouse?

Do you feel you could entrust the souls of your children to him or her should you pass on prematurely?

---

2. Francis, *Amoris Laetitia*, 71.

No person will ever complete us—only God can do that. That catchphrase "You complete me" is actually not true (sorry Hollywood fans). But God designed marriage for a reason and put a desire for it within our hearts. Marriage is a great mission work through which God wants to sanctify the world.

God absolutely does care who you marry.

Daily Challenge

Talk with your spouse about of the idea of "soul mates." What do you think about this? Do you think our ache for a soul mate is related to the fact that we are created in the image of God?

Prayer

God, be with us in our relationship. Allow our eyes to stay fixed on you so that we can grow together in holiness and friendship. Help us to trust in your plan.

✌

DAY THREE

Love the Person, Not the Idea

Love at first sight. We see it in romantic comedies and princess movies: two people see one other and everything stops or moves in slow motion. The lovers push past nameless strangers and confetti frozen in mid-air. The guy whispers in the woman's ear, they kiss, and then they ride off into the sunset.

We all know it doesn't work like this in the real world. How well did those two know each other, really? How much time did they spend together before running off? Did they attempt to take a three-hour road trip or assemble furniture together before they rode into the sunset forever and ever?

Deep, reverent love for a person doesn't happen instantaneously. Even Saint John Paul II says that the *eros* that draws us to another person is only the raw material of mature love—it's the kindling but it isn't a true fire yet. If we think *eros* is all there is to true love, it is very easy to allow our emotions to get away from us.

If we are blinded by our initial feelings of attraction, we may build up a person into something he or she is not. If we idealize (or idolize) the person we date, then the person we marry may seem like a completely different person. We can find ourselves jaded and cynical, if not outright hateful, toward the person for not measuring up to the perfect ideal we made them into. This is why there is wisdom in taking romantic matters slowly in order to allow the truth of the other person to be revealed.

We both know couples who fell in love with the idea of a person instead of the actual person, and it's a harsh reality. Sometimes the romance is more gripping than the reality of the relationship. A priest told us once that if true *agape* love is present, the reality should be *better* than the romance. We're not saying that there shouldn't be romance, but the reality of the person before us—with all their quirks, flaws, and shortcomings—should *increase* our love for them, not turn us off.

This is to love *totally*. To love in a total way is to accept everything that the person is and to help them on their way to holiness and greatness. To love totally is to go all in and embrace who our spouse *is*, not who we want them to be, and walk with them as a partner on this Christian journey.

Daily Challenge

Admit to your spouse something about him or her that bothers you (maybe they chew with their mouth open or put the toilet paper roll on the wrong way). Then discuss how in some way his or her reality as a whole person brings out the best in you.

Prayer

Lord, help us to see one another clearly and to love each other through and through.

❧

Day Four

Chastity and Dirty Windshields

Purity is a requirement of love. (*TOB* 49:7)

Do you feel a renewed desire to love your weird, quirky spouse in a total and life-giving way? When we acknowledge the goodness of the human body and learn the spousal meaning of the body, it ought to give us hope that it is possible to live a loving relationship with another person in a way that, these days, is countercultural.

So, hopefully you are now ready to hear about something that has fallen out of favor: chastity. To reclaim a truly Christian sense of *agape* love means to love with the virtue of chastity. If we rediscover this virtue, it will transform and integrate our desires and align our heads with our hearts.

What is chastity exactly? While it may conjure up images of a medieval belt with lock and key, the real meaning of chastity has nothing do with repression. Chastity begins as a discipline of the senses, heart, and body with the end goal of unselfish love. Chaste comes from the Latin word for "clean." To love chastely means to see the world and each person with clear (pure) vision.

If you've ever driven a dirty car and then finally make it to the carwash, you may have been astounded by how dirty your windshield was prior to the cleaning. You may have thought, "How did I not realize how dirty my car was?" We've all grown up with "filthy windshields," our visions clouded by false messages about the human body and the purpose of sexuality.

Real chastity pushes aside the false masks of prudishness or repressive puritanism, as well as the debasing animalism of our pornified hook-up culture. Chastity reclaims *awe* for God's creation, especially for the human body and how God is manifested through every inch and curve. Far from repression, chastity is like a white-hot fire that burns with rightly ordered *eros* and *agape* intertwined.

Saint John Paul II reminds us that "purity is the glory of the human body before God. It is the glory of God in the human body, through which masculinity and femininity are manifested" (*TOB* 57:3). Chastity frees our love from the stain of utilitarianism and the temptation to objectify others and use them as mere sources of pleasure.

A pure heart "lets us perceive the human body—ours and our neighbor's—as a temple of the Holy Spirit, a manifestation of divine beauty" (*CCC* 2519). Purity doesn't erase or repress our desires but hands them over—especially those that have become twisted and self-seeking—to Christ so that they can be made new and redirected.

The road of chaste love is a long journey that will be beset with setbacks and stumbling, but it is a path that leads to purification and transformation. Through Christ our desires can be untwisted and our vision can be wiped clean so that we may see in awe and wonder the beauty of the human person. Be patient with yourself in struggles and in times of lust. Christ entered into all sin and temptation so that we would have a guide to bring light into the darkness. Jesus assures us that chastity leads us to God: "Blessed are the pure in heart, for they will see God" (Mt 5:8).

Daily Challenge

Talk with your spouse about how you have understood the concept of "chastity" growing up. Do you understand chastity differently now? Are there any role models in your life who have lived a joyfully chaste lifestyle?

Prayer

Lord, give us pure eyes to see you. Give us a desire for chastity and the courage to reject all counterfeit love that tempts us from this path.

◦৯৶

Day Five

You Have Ravished My Heart

> You have ravished my heart, my sister, my bride, you have
> ravished my heart with a glance of your eyes. . . . How sweet
> is your love, my sister, my bride! (Sg 4:9–10)

How can a person grow in chastity? Many of us have
ingrained habits and ways of thinking that prevent of from seeing our spouse in a chaste way. Some of us may have grown up
with the understanding that the sexual act is "only for marriage"
and we were told nothing more about it. Some of us may have
"white knuckled" or repressed desires, which can lead to an
unhealthy focus on sex after we are married. Or we may have
spent many years engaging in sexual relationships outside of marriage and used other people for pleasure.

Sadly, these behaviors can lead to great hurt and abuse within
a marriage. A person should never be treated as an object to be
used, and this *especially* goes for our spouse. Marriage can never
be an outlet for our lust, because lust seeks to degrade and use the
beloved.

Saint John Paul II addresses this issue when he takes a seemingly strange turn in his great teaching to focus on the Song of
Songs, a book smack in the middle of our Sacred Scriptures.
Why? In short, he uses this beautiful book of erotic poetry to
exemplify the call of spousal love to echo that of brother and
sister.

You may be thinking, "What? A husband and wife loving each other as a brother and sister? Gross!"

If we remember the different types of love covered in Week 2, it may help us to understand John Paul II. To be tender with our spouse as if he or she were our sibling means to love our spouse with a complete *philia* and *agape* love. Without canceling any of the *eros* that draws spouses together, tender love always puts the good of the other first and turns from the temptation to lustfully use another person.

John Paul II uses the Song of Songs to illustrate how the bridegroom sees his bride as a *person* who shares with him a common humanity. The bridegroom in the Song of Songs, by calling his wife first "sister" before "bride," is seeking to "embrace her entire 'I,' soul and body, *with a disinterested tenderness*" (*TOB* 110:2).

This is a great challenge! We're not always taught to have such a noble love for our spouse. Instead we often believe our partner exists to satisfy our sexual fancies and whims. But to love one another as Christ calls us involves "initiation into the mystery of the person ... [without ever] implying the violation of that mystery" (*TOB* 111:1).

An essential exercise to grow in this disinterested love is to embrace praying with our spouse. In this vulnerability of prayer, "God penetrates the creature, who is completely 'naked' before him" (*TOB* 12:5, note 22).

Bobby: I believe that God planned that Jackie and I would be friends first before there was ever any romance. I was in the seminary, in formation for the diocesan priesthood, when we first met on a retreat devoted to learning and studying the theology of the body. In other circumstances we may have approached each other with different motives, but I was clearly "off limits," so that eliminated the possibility of romance for both of us.

This boundary enabled us to interact without any flirting or hidden agendas. We ate together at meals and learned about one another in a truly disinterested way, very much like brother and sister. She was in fact my sister in Christ. My own journey was (I thought) still directed to the priesthood, and I assumed she would one day meet a handsome, strapping, Catholic guy, most likely with a beard. We kept a casual conversation going about once every four or five months, but neither of us was on the other's radar.

A year and a half later, I was in the process of leaving the seminary because I felt called by God to the married vocation. Jackie and I met once again and, much to our surprise, God made it very clear that our love was ready to bloom. I was the bearded Catholic guy all along!

I am so thankful to God for giving us both clarity, right discernment, and the courage to pursue what had been revealed in his time. Because we built a friendship first, I could truly look at Jackie as a "sister" first and allow romance to supplement that essential foundation of friendship.

Daily Challenge

Prepare an environment (living room, patio, etc.) as a space for prayer. Perhaps light a candle or place a crucifix between you. Begin by asking the Holy Spirit to teach you how to pray and to see one another as God sees his beloved children.

Prayer

Father, help us to love one another with reverence and awe, so we can grow in real friendship and tenderness and always exclaim, "How beautiful you are, my love, how very beautiful!" (Sg 4:1).

༄

DAY SIX

Masters of Our Own Mystery

> A garden locked is my sister, my bride, a garden locked, a
> fountain sealed. (Sg 4:12)

If you've ever barged into a sibling's room or read someone else's diary (or maybe someone else read *yours*), you know what it feels like to intrude upon the intimate space of another person. Or maybe you lived through the horror of one of the worst teenage punishments when your parents removed the door of your room and you felt an utter lack of privacy.

No one should invade the inner intimacy of another. Saint John Paul II notes how the imagery of the Song of Songs illustrates this, "The bride appears to the eyes of the bridegroom as a 'garden closed' and 'fountain sealed' . . . [because the] bride *presents herself to the eyes of the man as the master of her own mystery*" (*TOB* 110:7). This is true for both parties in a relationship: we are all "masters of our own mystery."

Authentic love is always *free* and never coerced or manipulated. If a person violates his or her beloved (emotionally or physically) it is not love at all. Abusive relationships, built on a false understanding of mutual submission (see Day 2 of Week 3), are not in God's plan of love.

Love can only be freely entrusted to a person who has earned our trust. The risk, of course, is that love can be rejected. Perhaps no one has put it more eloquently than C. S. Lewis:

> To love at all is to be vulnerable. Love anything and your heart will be wrung and possibly broken. If you want to make sure of keeping it intact you must give it to no one, not even an animal. Wrap it carefully round with hobbies and little luxuries; avoid all entanglements. Lock it up safe in the casket or coffin of your selfishness. But in that casket, safe, dark, motionless, airless, it will change. It will not be broken; it will become unbreakable, impenetrable, irredeemable.[3]

Some people refrain from displaying love for fear of rejection, others experience rejection so they avoid being vulnerable again. But to do so is to lose the essential nature of love's total gift.

Jesus models the supreme display of vulnerability in the total, free gift of himself on the Cross: "No one takes it from me, but I lay it down on my own" (Jn 10:18). Jesus offered himself naked, freely, and totally on the Cross that redeemed the world, and in each and every Mass his sacrifice is reaffirmed: "This is my body, which is given for you" (Lk 22:19). Jesus shows us that love enters darkness and takes on suffering in order to offer a free gift "in good times and bad, in sickness and health, until death do us part" (although, as we will see tomorrow, even death does not have the final say).

If love truly is patient and kind, then we must always be willing to put to death the selfish tendencies that can injure love (see 1 Cor 13:4). Jesus gave us the model: "This is my body, which is given for you" (Lk 22:9).

Let's pick up our crosses to live this out.

---

3. Lewis, *The Four Loves*, 121.

Daily Challenge

Take to prayer the times your trust in another person has been misplaced or abused, when you may have been rejected, or perhaps when you violated the trust of another person. In prayer, give any past hurts to God for healing.

Prayer

Lord, help us to be vulnerable, to protect one another's privacy, and to love openly and with great freedom. Help us to respect one another's intimate space while at the same time opening the mystery of ourselves as much as possible:

Set me as a seal upon your heart,
as a seal upon your arm;
for love is strong as death,
passion fierce as the grave.
Its flashes are flashes of fire,
a raging flame.

Song of Songs 8:6

᷌

Day Seven

The Test of Virtuous Love

Sarah was the unluckiest bride known to man. The Book of Tobit tells the story of a woman who married seven men, one after the other. Each man died in the bridal chamber on the wedding night *before* the unlucky couple was able to consummate their marriage (see Tob 6:14).

The angel Raphael then appears to a young man named Tobias and tells him to marry Sarah. (Yeah, yikes!) Raguel, Sarah's father, warns Tobias of his probable fate, but he gives Tobias permission to marry his daughter and says, "May the Lord of heaven, my child, guide and prosper you both this night and grant you mercy and peace" (Tob 7:11). Quite humorously, Raguel later goes off to dig Tobias' early grave, expecting Tobias to die in the same manner as Sarah's other suitors. (It's not a stretch for most husbands to imagine their fathers-in-law delightfully digging their early graves).

But Tobias is not afraid; he chooses to walk courageously into the den of evil. Tobias is able to make this choice because he trusts in the power of God:

> The truth and the strength of love are manifested in the ability of [love] to place itself between the forces of good and of evil that fight within man and around him, because love is confident in the victory of good and is ready to do everything in order that good may conquer. (*TOB* 115:2)

Love is stronger than death. The risk that Tobias takes foreshadows the spousal offering of Christ on the Cross and calls us all to face our own selfishness and lust, to bear our crosses, and to march confidently in the face of fear because death does not have the final say. "Where, O death, is your victory? Where, O death, is your sting?" (1 Cor 15:55). Christ rose from the dead! Authentic Love has conquered all sin, ugliness, and even death.

Even though the Book of Tobit was written before the coming of Christ, Tobias is confident that God can conquer death. On their wedding night, in the face of evil, Tobias leads Sarah in prayer with these beautiful words:

> Blessed are you, O God of our ancestors,
> and blessed is your name in all generations forever.
> Let the heavens and the whole creation bless you forever.
> You made Adam, and for him you made his wife, Eve,
> as a helper and support.
> From the two of them the human race has sprung.
> You said, "It is not good that the man should be alone;
> let us make a helper for him like himself."
> I now am taking this kinswoman of mine,
> not because of lust,
> but with sincerity.
> Grant that she and I may find mercy
> and that we may grow old together.

Tobit 8:5–8

The prayer of Tobias with Sarah is an echo of the promise couples make to one another on their wedding day and the proposal that Christ offers us all: "I will love you and honor you all the days of my life."

Daily Challenge

Pray the prayer of Tobias and Sarah with each other tonight. Pray it slowly and with reverence.

Prayer

Lord, help us to love one another "until death do us part" and beyond. Like Sarah and Tobit, may we love and honor each other all the days of our life.

WEEK FIVE

What Endangers Our Love?

Day One

The Shadow of Sin

We live in a painfully fallen world. Modern dating and the hook-up culture foster self-centered, careless relationships that often end in heartache. Use, abuse, divorce, and pornography are prevalent. Most relationships are far from having fairy-tale endings. As we all know, the great vision of spousal love as an image of the Trinity often falls short in the *lived* reality.

Saint John Paul II recognized that the human ideal has been impacted by original sin. Adam and Eve were "*original man*" but now we are "*historical man*"—unique, contemporary human beings born into a state of broken union with God our Father. We were not born in the Garden of Eden but on the battlefield of good and evil. Sin—the separation from God and his love—is the reality of our lives, and it wreaks havoc from one generation to the next. While God originally intended for us to live forever (both bodily and spiritually), the introduction of sin into the world brought both spiritual and physical death (see Rom 6:23).

The first sin of disobedience was the *original sin* that ruptured our relationship with God, creation, one another, and our very selves. When original man and woman listened to the lies of evil and began to question God's goodness, John Paul II called this, "*the key moment in which, in man's heart, doubt is cast on the Gift*" (*TOB* 26:4). Suddenly God was no longer seen as a loving, benevolent Father, but as a tyrant who withholds greatness from man and woman.

The serpent (Satan) tempted Eve to doubt God's love as a Father, and this doubt persists today in both women and men. The "Father of Lies," as Satan is sometimes called, still tries to convince us that we are not good enough and delights when we forget that we are God's beloved sons and daughters. Instead of receiving the love and fulfillment that only God can provide, we can suffer from a deep fear of being forever alone, which can lead to a grasping for loves other than God.

Adam's great sin was his refusal to stand between the evil one and his beloved. Adam "who was with her" the entire time in the Garden, never spoke up to defend Eve during the entire exchange with Satan (Gen 3:6). His sin of silence continues to plague humanity, inclining us to avoid adversity because of selfishness or cowardice.

This week's reflections will examine the shadow of sin cast on us all, clouding our ability to give and receive love. These topics are not the most cheerful, but it is a necessary journey. Before we arrive at Easter Sunday, we must first pass through Good Friday. Even when we do not want to acknowledge the wounds or the hurts we've sustained from past relationships (or the hurt we may have inflicted on others), no real healing can begin unless we allow Christ into the darkness of our sin.

Christ always appeals to the "inner man," to the healing of our hearts where real conversion is possible. We don't need to hide our sinful hearts, as Adam and Eve did, for Christ already knows our sinfulness and beckons us to leave behind our fears and our selfishness.

Have the courage to turn to prayer often during this week, especially if the readings stir up any painful memories or guilt. When we are vulnerable with God and bring all things to his light, that's when healing begins.

Daily Challenge

Consider how you may have doubted God's love and plans for you. Perhaps you struggle with feeling unworthy or not good enough. Reflect on the times you've tried to grasp for love instead of waiting on what God wanted to reveal to you. Share any insights with your spouse.

Prayer

God, you have created us as your sons and daughters full of worth, dignity, and goodness. Help us to know that while we are good, we have often fallen short. Give us the courage to see these weaknesses and have hope that in you we may be made new again. May we truly believe that "if anyone is in Christ, there is a new creation: everything old has passed away; see; everything has become new!" (2 Cor 5:17). Make us new creations!

༄

Day Two

The Opposite of Love

> You have heard that it was said, "You shall not commit adultery." But I say to you that everyone who looks at a woman with lust has already committed adultery with her in his heart. (Mt 5:27–28)

Ever since sin was introduced into the human story, we struggle to see one another with the eyes of original innocence. Our God-given *eros* and desire for beauty has turned inward for selfish reasons. Our first reaction to the human body is often not one of love and innocent wonder, but one of lust. The human body is no longer seen as a sacred *gift* to be cherished, but as an *object* to be used.

Indeed, in the mid-twentieth century in his book *Love and Responsibility*, Saint John Paul II predicted that in the future the opposite of love would not be *hate* but *use*. To use another person as an object is to disregard the unique, unrepeatable gift they are and focus solely on the pleasure they provide.

This *utilitarian view of personhood*—that a person's worth is connected with their usefulness—is the cultural air we breathe. Many think, "If an older person is suffering and no longer of much use to us, isn't euthanasia the 'caring' option? If an unexpected child threatens our plans or is simply inconvenient, why not consider abortion? What's wrong with using another person for a hook-up or one-night stand? Why not look at pornography and use the image of another person for mere pleasure?"

If we have to choose between pleasure and pain, or what demands less and what costs more, we know which one we are more inclined to choose. John Paul II observed: "The 'heart' has become a battlefield between love and concupiscence. The more concupiscence dominates the heart, the less the heart experiences the spousal meaning of the body" (*TOB* 32:3).

This theological term "concupiscence" (*con-CUE-pah-sense*) refers to the disordering of our passions that afflicts us all due to our fallen nature. While not a sin in itself, concupiscence is an *inclination to sin* that encourages us to selfishly seek pleasure for ourselves, even at the cost of using another person.

So, what is the solution or the response to concupiscence? John Paul II points to the words of Christ at the Sermon on the Mount (quoted earlier) as an invitation, not to impossible demands, but to transforming love: man and woman "*must rediscover the lost fullness of . . . [their] humanity and want to regain it*" (*TOB* 43:7).

No person was ever meant to be used, abused, or thrown away. Jesus "assigns the dignity of every woman as a task to every man . . . he assigns also the dignity of every man to every woman" (*TOB* 100:6). He calls every man and woman to look at the entire person before them, not as a collection of body parts to be used for pleasure, but as a unique and unrepeatable child of God.

The saints, the holiest of men and women, knew that their hearts *constantly* needed purification. Rather than stifling disordered desires or pretending they didn't exist, the saints handed them over to be transformed by the grace of God. While we shouldn't beat ourselves up or become overly scrupulous when we have lustful thoughts, we absolutely need to embrace purification in order to begin the process of *integration*.

What does this chaste integration look like? In moments of temptation we can offer up our thoughts to God. A quick prayer, "Lord help me to see the beauty of this person," or "God, please allow this man or woman to know their goodness and their worth." When we do this, God will give us the grace to see the whole person and disordered desires will gradually be untwisted.

Sin is not natural to man—love is. It *is* possible to turn from looking at each other with the eyes of lust. But rather than just following external rules, real change will require internal transformation. It's a lifelong journey, but thanks be to God that he walks with us along each step of the way.

Daily Challenge

Who are some of the people in your life who you have used for emotional or physical pleasure? When have you been used or let yourself be used by someone? Have you ever seen someone's worth by whether or not they were "useful" to you? Share these things, however difficult, with your spouse.

Prayer

Lord, help us to see every human being as created in your image and likeness. We are sorry for the ways we have used others for our own physical and emotional pleasure. We are sorry for any times we have let others use us. Heal our bodies, so they may be your hands and feet. Heal our minds, so we might think of holy things and have renewed memories. Heal our hearts, so that they may be pure. Heal our souls, so that we may become saints.

❧

Day Three

Guarding the Gift

The marital embrace between man and woman is natural and good, but most of us have a sense that it is *not* natural for a third party to be present in the room. We're inclined to shield ourselves from onlookers who have no right to see our naked bodies or to witness the holy exchange of husband and wife.

There is something sacred between a couple who has vowed to love one another totally, and the nakedness between the two is a bodily sign of vulnerability and trust. As Saint John Paul II says in *Love and Responsibility*, "shame becomes in a sense absorbed by love, melted in it."[1]

However, shame never completely disappears in a couple's relationship, and that's a good thing! Today many hear the word "shame" and view it in a negative way. We often associate it with guilt. However, John Paul II believes that shame is "a natural self-defense of the person against descending or being pushed into the position of an object."[2] He writes that, "shame has a two-fold meaning: it indicates the threat to the value [of the person] and at the same time preserves this value in an interior way" (*TOB* 28:6).

---

1. Wojtyla, *Love and Responsibility*, 165.
2. Ibid., 166.

Thus, John Paul II is saying *not* that the body is bad and needs to be covered, but that the body is *so* good that it needs to be protected from anyone who would potentially use or abuse it (or not love it in its fullness).

Here's an example: When you exit the shower in front of your spouse, there may be no particular rush to cover up; but, if a random stranger happened to be there at the wrong place and wrong time, you would grab the towel more quickly than the speed of light.

Adam and Eve were "naked without shame" in the Garden of Eden. But, when sin entered the world, shame also entered the world. If we all still lived in the Garden of Eden in "original nakedness," we wouldn't need to cover up or protect ourselves from lust, because *lust wouldn't exist*. However, we live in a fallen world where *lust does exist* and people are inclined to view each other as objects of use rather than persons to be loved. (This is why nudist colonies will sadly always be more creepy than beautiful.)

Thus, we only reveal the *fullness* of who we are (both bodily and spiritually) to our spouse: to the one who has promised to love us freely, totally, faithfully, and fruitfully. Shame thus serves as a positive experience that attempts to guard and protect what should only be seen by our spouse.

As we discussed yesterday, love always waits on the beloved. We may have past hurts or wounds that center on our bodies, and we may find it awkward, difficult, or scary to reveal ourselves wholly to our spouse. This must be met with patience and tenderness by a spouse and a willingness to put him or herself in the other's shoes. Love never forces or intrudes, but waits for the person to reveal the gift of himself or herself.

Shame still serves a purpose today. Rightly understood, shame helps us guard the gift of our personhood to reserve it for our beloved alone. Tomorrow we will examine how the effects of sin have attempted to thwart the creative energy that God willed to share with us—our fertility.

Daily Challenge

Share with your spouse a time when you felt like you needed to protect yourself from the glance of someone else. Then share what it is about your spouse that makes you feel comfortable and loved enough to be fully naked in front of him or her.

Prayer

God, we thank you for the gift of one another. Thank you for our love and how we are comfortable in one another's presence. Help us to have a renewed sense of wonder for our spouse's body, even as we age and know each other more and more.

ॐ

Day Four

Babies and Bonding

We've all heard the phrase: "Make sure you protect yourself." Protect ourselves from what? Bears? Ninjas? Robots? None of the above. Certainly, the push for safe sex includes protection from sexually transmitted diseases, but so often babies get lumped into that group of nasty things to avoid. The "responsible" thing, we are told, is to avoid the very outcome for which sexual union was designed: to create babies.

When a woman conceives a child, it's not that something went *wrong*, but that something went very *right*!

Without a doubt, one of the hardest teachings of the Church for people to accept today is her stance against contraception. But if you've been on board with us up to this point regarding the beauty of the human person and our divine call to love, then please give this idea a chance. This challenging teaching, which is in no way antiscience or irrational, makes sense in light of what the theology of the body teaches us regarding the spousal meaning of the body and the call to be selflessly creative in the image and likeness of God.

The Church teaches that there are two ends to the sexual union between a husband and wife in marriage: *babies* and *bonding*. The marital embrace unifies and bonds the man and woman together in a deeper union, while it is also geared toward the procreation and education of children. But what we have today is the rupture between babies and bonding—unbridled and self-seeking *eros* wants the bonding (and the pleasure that comes from it), but not the babies.

The very first commandment of God to his people, as we stated earlier, was: "Be fruitful and multiply" (Gen 1:28). God, an interpersonal communion of life and love, desires for us to be *co-creators* in the life of love. But in our fallen state we're tempted to view this ability to generate new life as a burden and not a supreme gift.

Children used to be seen as a great gift for a family, but now, especially in the West, children are seen as an encumbrance to freedom. You better believe that raising a child is a fatiguing endeavor. In our own family, we have experienced the exhaustion, but we have also experienced how our children sanctify us. There is no greater joy in the world than to be parents who are entrusted with another little soul.

(See our Appendix on Natural Family Planning to learn more about the natural method of fertility monitoring and the Church's call to responsible parenthood.)

Jackie: When I was eighteen, I went to a week-long retreat with thirty other high school teens that changed my life. During the all-girls' session, one of our female leaders shared how she and her fiancé were learning about Natural Family Planning (NFP) so they could prayerfully discern the times to achieve or avoid pregnancy during marriage.

While all the other teen girls nodded their heads with enthusiasm, I was very uncomfortable. I felt stupid. Here I was a Catholic for my whole life and no one ever told me that contraception in marriage was a sin.

I thought that it was a normal thing to be on "the Pill" once you got married. Even though I had decided to wait until marriage to have sex (since I had learned that pre-marital sex was a sin, and I didn't want to get pregnant before marriage or end up with an STD), I thought you could do whatever you wanted in marriage, and the Pill was an obvious way to avoid having fifty children.

When I got home from that retreat, I immersed myself in what the Catholic Church actually taught regarding contraception. Originally, I was skeptical. I thought this teaching was about giving us more rules that no one could or would actually obey. But, as I read through Pope Paul VI's encyclical *Humanae Vitae* (Of Human Life), where the teachings on contraception were explained, my heart leapt. I thought, "Wow! This is so beautiful! I can't believe a 2000-year-old Church founded by Jesus Christ and led by the Holy Spirit actually knows more than me, an eighteen-year-old!" I laugh at that realization now, but, as I kept learning, I realized that the Church teaches what it does because it wants the best for me. The Church wants me not only to love rightly, but also to be loved rightly, especially in my marriage!

Sure, it was attractive to me that couples who practice Natural Family Planning in their marriage have a less than two percent divorce rate. It was also attractive that NFP (which scientifically centers around the woman's body) encourages a husband to tenderly love his wife, not only by being in awe that "woman" is made with such complexity and beauty, but also through finding ways to love her other than sex, especially when times of abstinence are called for.

If God is the author of love, and you leave God out of the bedroom, what do you have left?

Daily Challenge

Share with your spouse how you were raised to think about contraception. What was your family's attitude toward it? How do you feel about the Church's teaching on contraception? Is there anything you can do together to learn more about the Church's teaching?

Prayer

God, open our ears to hear, our eyes to see, our hearts to your goodness. Help us to be open to life-giving love, even when it makes us uncomfortable. May we always include you, who are Love, in our lives, especially in our most intimate moments.

DAY FIVE

Desires of a Twisted Eros

We live in a pornographic culture. We are constantly inundated with images that objectify the body—in particular, the female body—to market entertainment and sell products. Images that would have scandalized our grandparents are commonplace today, whether it's online or in supermarket magazine racks. The prevalence and perversity of pornography has grown bolder and more violent with each passing year.

Statistics today show that the average age of first exposure to Internet pornography is very young, between the ages of nine and eleven. An innocent search gone wrong can mean that a young person is exposed to some of the worst depravity possible. Whether male or female, we all have been affected by what porn has done to the world. We're all the walking wounded in some way.

It has been said that the problem with pornography is not that it shows too much, but that it shows too little. In pornography we see only a body, but not a body *and* a soul, a unique and unrepeatable human person. We see a body to lust after, but not someone's daughter or sister or son or brother who deserves to be loved with tenderness. Our passionate *eros* desires are good, we must remember, but a warped and destructive form of *eros* love dehumanizes us all.

The grave distortions of sex surround us, but they are not insurmountable. Saint John Paul II was unwilling to throw in the towel in the struggle for the human heart: "The spousal meaning of the body has not become totally foreign to the human heart: *it has not been totally suffocated in it by concupiscence, but only habitually threatened....* Does this mean that we should distrust the human heart? No! It is only to say that we must remain in control of it" (*TOB* 32:3).

We all need healing and a discerning heart when it comes to understanding the movements of our heart and the kinds of love (or distortions of love) we are feeling or experiencing. Instead of repressing or indulging in the desires of a twisted *eros*, we are called to allow God's love to flood our hearts so that we can be transformed and redeemed.

Bobby: I was about twelve years old when I first stumbled upon pornography for the first time. My uncle had a stack of *Playboy* magazines in his closet that was as big as I was. By the time I entered college, the Internet—which used to be a slow, dial-up ordeal—became a high-speed battleground. Now every phone, tablet, and computer was an opportunity for temptation.

Thanks to God I found a solid group of guys through the college campus ministry and later in seminary. We supported, encouraged, and challenged one another. Thankfully, I was porn-free for several years before meeting Jackie, and it was a gift to enter marriage truly free from porn. It's my privilege to now journey with young men who also want to love rightly and want all counterfeit loves—especially porn—out of their lives.

Don't be afraid to go to confession again and again and again, even if for the same sins. These struggles in chastity usually stem from loneliness, stress, or deeper issues we need to address. In the confessional we meet the merciful Jesus, not any individual priest. Own your sin and trust in the healing power of Christ: "Lord, I am not worthy to have you come under my roof; but only speak the word, and my servant will be healed" (Mt 8:8).

Pope Francis said beautifully, "God never tires of forgiving us; we are the ones who tire of seeking his mercy."[3]

Daily Challenge

Talk to your spouse about the times you may have viewed or treated other people as objects (including exposure to pornography). Listen to one another compassionately and be merciful if you have not struggled with this issue. Have the courage to admit if you need help, and continue to pray together for healing in this area.

Prayer

God, please heal any distorted images we have seen and untwist the lies that have been planted in our hearts. Help us to reclaim a sense of wonder that respects the dignity of the human body and send any lustful desires to the foot of the Cross.

---

3. Francis, *Evangelii Gaudium* [Apostolic Exhortation on the Proclamation of the Gospel in Today's Word], Vatican Web site, November 24, 2013, sec. 3, accessed Nov. 3, 2016, http://w2.vatican.va/content/francesco/en/apost_exhortations/documents/papa-francesco_esortazione-ap_20131124_evangelii-gaudium.html, November 24, 2013, sec. 3.

❦

Day Six

The Healing Power of Confession

In case we're tempted to be too hard on ourselves for any past mistakes or failures in living authentic love, we must remember that *we are all fallen*. We all need a Savior.

Maybe you're reading this and have not struggled with these issues as much as other people, even your spouse. Awesome! But if you have a sexual past, have viewed pornography, have used contraception, entertained any lustful thoughts, or carry any darkness of sin with you, that sin absolutely needs to go. Sin clouds our vision and inhibits our ability to *see* and *live* this great spousal meaning of the body.

Christ came to restore us to life and to bring genuine healing to our bodies *and* our souls. As Catholics, we believe that Christ gave the amazing ability to forgive sins (something that only God can do) to his priests (see Mt 18:18 and Jn 20:22–23) and that gift continues through today.

Our sin is never too big for God to forgive, and no one is ever so far gone to return home to the Father's embrace. Perhaps it's been years since your last confession; perhaps you had a bad experience in confession with a particular priest and that has forever colored your experience of this sacrament; perhaps you're just afraid.

Pope Francis, the "pope of mercy" as some have called him, affirmed the simplicity of the sacrament: "Confessing our sins is not going to a psychiatrist, or to a torture chamber: it's saying to the Lord: 'Lord, I am a sinner.'"[4] Confession breaks the chains that our sin has over us. It won't immediately cure a habit built up over years, but the sacrament absolutely frees us to begin anew with abundant grace. Saint Paul wrote: "But you were washed, you were sanctified, you were justified in the name of the Lord Jesus Christ and in the Spirit of our God" (1 Cor 6:11).

Bobby: Saint John Paul II went to confession weekly. What he had to confess, only God knows! Making a date to go to confession as a couple (but not at the same time!) can be a renewing, healing experience. We try to go to confession once a month, confessing even the "little" sins of impatience, gossip, and sloth. We get a feeling of lightness after a good confession. Our souls feel unburdened as we leave sin-free (until we drive away into California traffic . . . then anger returns).

Saint John Vianney was a parish priest who lived in France in the nineteenth century. He transformed his small, backwater town because of his holy example—some days he heard confessions for up to sixteen hours. He knew the healing and transforming power of the sacrament, and he once said that we should not wallow in guilt but should rather "wallow in the mercy of God."

God is always calling us to start anew and to be transformed through the graces of confession. If you feel invited to live the

---

4. "Pope Francis: confess sins with concreteness and sincerity," Vatican Radio, last updated October 25, 2013, http://en.radiovaticana.va/storico/2013/10/25/pope_francis_confess_sins_with_concreteness_and_sincerity/en1-740557.

spousal meaning of the body, but you need to dust off your soul from these sins that weigh you down, there's no better place to start than through the grace of the Sacrament of Reconciliation.

Daily Challenge

If it has been a long time since your last confession, check out your local parish's availability. Resolve to receive the sacrament sometime when you have time (consider making the trip to your parish as a couple). Encourage one another to receive the sacrament when you are able.

Prayer

Lord, may we always run to you when our sin gets the best of us. Help us to trust that you are a loving Father who always welcomes us home.

cઋ

Day Seven

The Cross of Redemption

While it may be tempting to despair and dwell on our sins and unworthiness, we shouldn't forget some of the essential facts of our faith: God sent his only Son so that we might be set free; Christ died so that we may have life and life in abundance; through the Cross he has redeemed the world.

If you've ever been to a carnival or a bowling alley gift shop, you know that you have to trade in worthless tickets to redeem a prize of real worth (which is still relatively worthless). To *redeem* is essentially to gain possession of something in exchange for a payment.

We have been redeemed. Jesus has paid the price for our sins with his life (1 Cor 6:20) so that we might gain possession of heaven (Phil 3:12–14). THIS is Good News! We deserve death by our sins, but Jesus redeems us, taking our place on the Cross to give us new life.

We can grow up our entire lives going to Mass, receiving the sacraments, and staring at the crucifix, and yet never consciously realize that Jesus actually gave his life as redemption for our sin. When people have "wake up" or conversion experiences, they often feel great remorse and cry bitter tears because it finally sinks in that God has paid off their debts with the blood of his own Son:

> Christ is God's final word on this subject; in fact, the covenant established with him and through him between God

and humanity opens an infinite perspective of Life: and access to the Tree of Life—according to the original plan of the God of the covenant—is revealed to every man in its definitive fullness. This will be the meaning of Christ's death and resurrection; this will be the testimony of the paschal mystery. (*TOB* 65:6)

Through his *bodily* suffering and death on the Cross, Jesus took our sins and showed us that through embracing suffering and the crosses we've borne (be it abuse, pornography, unhealthy relationships, etc.), we can all be made new. Jesus is the great healer of bodies and souls—the great healer of humanity.

When we commit to live the spousal meaning of our bodies, it means dying to our "old selves" so that we can put on Christ and become "new creations" (see Gal 3:27; 2:20). "*At the center of the mystery is Christ* . . . [T]he men and women who accept through faith the gift offered to them in Christ really become sharers in the eternal mystery" (*TOB* 94:5).

While the content of this past week may have stirred up some painful memories or touched wounds that still throb, Christ desires for us to allow him to enter into our hearts and heal us. God is a gentleman. He will never barge into our lives uninvited and waits on our initiative. He proposes his love to us on the Cross.

How will we respond?

Daily Challenge

Take a few minutes to meditate on this essential mystery of faith— that God redeemed the entire human race through the blood of his

Son. Jesus Christ redeemed YOU! Talk this out with your spouse. Do you really believe it? What does it mean for your life, and your marriage, if you believe that this is true?

Prayer

Jesus, thank you for paying the price, for giving your life so that we may be set free from our sins. You have given us everything—may we give you everything in return and say "Yes" to your divine proposal. Nothing would be better than to spend eternity with you!

> I love you, O my God, and my only desire is to love you until the last breath of my life. I love you, O my infinitely lovable God, and I would rather die loving you, than live without loving you. I love you, Lord, and the only grace I ask is to love you eternally. . . . My God, if my tongue cannot say in every moment that I love you, I want my heart to repeat it to you as often as I draw breath.[5]

---

5. Saint John Vianney, as quoted in the *Catechism of the Catholic Church*, no. 2658.

What Is God's Plan for Our Family?

❧

Day One

Society's Foundational Building Block

We've now laid the foundation of this great vision of the human person, the goodness of our embodiment as male and female, and we have recognized the dangers in the battlefield against sin. We now revisit the crucial call *to be creative* just as we have been created in God's image. The foundational building block of our society lies at the heart of this creative energy: the family.

We all have biological parents and an earthly family as well as a heavenly family. We have been created in the image of God's Trinitarian love, and this is why we're not meant for solitude, but for communion. The family is where we begin to make sense of these truths because it is an earthly image of our eternal end.

No family is perfect—we all know and have experienced that reality. Family is often the crucible where faults, failures, and shortcomings rise to the surface and are dealt with, either healthily or unhealthily. The way we experience and live in our family has consequences.

"As the family goes, so goes the nation and so goes the whole world in which we live," Saint John Paul II declared during a pilgrimage to Australia.[1] He understood all too well the dangers present to the family—dangers from without and from within. Our own sinfulness or upbringing can obscure our vision of family and stifle our generosity. Governments that seek to redefine the essential nature of marriage have lost the biblical understanding (and even the biological sense) of what it means to be male and to be female, particularly how the sexes balance each other in their complementarity and create the most suitable environment for the next generation.

The call to be *fruitful* can be scary, but, as John Paul II reminded us over and over again, "Be not afraid!" God redeemed the world *through the human body*, and *through our bodies* we can be temples of the Holy Spirit, temples of grace and peace for a world still divided. Through marriage, God allows us to participate in bringing the kingdom of heaven to earth. We are co-creators, involved in bringing new, immortal, and unrepeatable souls into the world through the care of a family.

Our God became a child. The God of the universe entrusted himself to a human family! Mary, though free of sin, and Joseph, a virtuous man, likely experienced all the frustrations, stresses, and joys of family life. Jesus was obedient to his parents and showed us how God puts the human family at the center of his drama of grace conquering sin.

---

1. John Paul II, *Homily in Perth*, Vatican Web site, November 30, 1986, accessed Nov. 3, 2016, https://w2.vatican.va/content/john-paul-ii/en/homilies/1986/documents/hf_jp-ii_hom_19861130_perth-australia.html.

We have been created in God's image—a communion of persons. This is why the family is the ordinary way that we are led to have a meaningful human existence. We were born into a family, and we are called to continue to be fruitful, bear life, and be open to participating in this amazing mission given to us by God.

Daily Challenge

Share some details and struggles you have had within your family. Also share any unique family traditions. Plan potential new traditions you would like to maintain in your future family, as well as goals for praying together.

Prayer

Dear Jesus, we humbly implore you to grant your special graces to our family. May our home be a shrine of peace, purity, love, labor, and faith. We beg you to protect and bless all of us, absent and present, living and dead.

❧

Day Two

Communion of Persons

Watching a couple dance—a couple who *really* knows how to dance—is a beautiful thing to behold. The hours of practice and endless repetition that goes into good dancing are not obvious because couples that are good at dancing exude effortlessness. Whether ballroom, foxtrot, tango, or swing, a great dancing couple communicates without words. They know how to lead and to be led, and appreciate the tension that keeps them together.

We love dancing together. While we have children who now dictate our sleep schedules and overall sanity, we still try to dance regularly (even in our own room if we can't go out). We make mistakes and we step on each other's toes, but our dancing reminds us that we're in this dance of life together.

One of the first things you learn when dancing is that there must be *tension* between you and your partner. Not awkward tension, but true physical tension—you have to grip your partner with a degree of torque, and movements are taut for the sake of momentum. You don't move each other passively, but with strength and purpose. This brings the dance to life and creates a greater energy than you have alone. Dancing unites us.

As we noted in earlier weeks, the notion that couples "complete" one other is a popular sentiment. One often hears things like, "She is my better half." However, only God can truly *complete* us in the proper sense, and no human person can ever satisfy all the longings of our heart. But there is *also* the great truth that man and woman are meant to complement one another as a "communion of persons" (or in Latin *communio personarum*).

Saint John Paul II emphasized that the *communio* dimension of the human person is key to understanding our identity and mission as human beings. We find meaning only in and through relationships with others: "It is not good that the man should be alone; I will make him a helper as his partner" (Gen 2:18). Man's original solitude and aloneness in the world is joyfully shattered when he discovers his "other" in the woman. Male and female become an image of God when their love is joined. Our *communion* as male and female joins us and brings out the best in one another.

Men and women make sense of one another's existence. The bodies of men and women demonstrate the great truth of complementarity in that they actually fit together like puzzle pieces—one body physically gives while the other body is meant to receive. Side by side our bodies make sense—alone we do not.

This unity between the husband and the wife doesn't end in itself but should always lead to an openness to the creation of new life by establishing a family. This *communio* is thus always life-giving, a direct imaging of God whose love overflows. This great rhythm of love and of creative life is the music that animates us and, like a partner beckoning us to the dance floor, God wants us to participate in the dance.

Daily Challenge

Dance this week with your spouse. You can either go out someplace or put on some music at home. Look into one another's eyes while you dance and try to anticipate the movements of the other. (Remember to laugh!)

Prayer

Lord, help us to understand our deep call to communion. Let us appreciate the way we complement one another and bless us with many years to participate in this dance of life together.

Day Three

Miracles of Creation

Babies are awesome.

But these days, children are not regarded as a universal good. Most of us are taught to fear the prospect of children because of the demands they place on us. Contraception may have been thrown at you in college (condoms were literally *thrown* on us during a health assembly). We've been taught to seek the pleasures of the sexual union without the "consequences."

But if true love is diffusive and by its very nature overflowing, shouldn't children be a part of our marriage?

"Since God is goodness, and goodness tends to diffuse itself, God hates voluntary barrenness and sterility," Archbishop Fulton Sheen wrote. "God will ask each person on judgment day: 'Where are your children?'"[2]

To one's surprise, Fulton Sheen was actually directing this question toward celibate men and women. Those who have voluntarily chosen a celibate vocation—the priests, brothers, sisters, or consecrated single people you may know—have taken a vow to remain unmarried, but *have not* rejected the call to bear life. They are *spiritually* fruitful. We call a priest "father" for a reason, and any priest will tell you that he has many, many spiritual

---

2. Sheen, *Three to Get Married*, 111.

children. Likewise, we both know many selfless youth ministers, catechists, and other lay servants who have no biological children but give of their time and energy like any parent would.

Love is always *incarnational*. Love seeks to become concrete. We give gifts, flowers, photo albums, and chocolates to our beloved, but the greatest gift of all is new life itself. Remember that marriage is an icon of the Trinity. The Holy Spirit is the *Lord and Giver of Life*, who directly proceeds from the Father and the Son. We cannot be a model of authentic love without being open to new life. This is why an integral part of saying, "I do" in the Catholic Church is a posture open to children.

But even more profoundly, as man and woman we get to be "co-creators" with God in bearing new life. Of course, only God can *will* a soul into creation and breathe life into a new person, but as humans we contribute our biological raw material to the process and pray for God to bless it. Every child conceived is the miraculous result of creative love!

Our own children are miracles of creation. We can see our genetics or personality traits in them, but they are wholly new and unrepeatable individuals. They are sassy, cuddly, strong-willed goofballs. It is hard for most married couples to imagine life without their children once they arrive. They humble us and make us less selfish. Are they an inconvenience? You bet. But every poopy diaper and hour of lost sleep provides an opportunity to embrace the Cross and leads us into a greater and more selfless love.

It's helpful to remember that we were all once children who made messes, threw tantrums, and made great demands on those who raised us. As our parents had to be patient with us, so we must pass on this love. If God truly wills to give us the gift of children, how can we refuse? What greater gift to a marriage could there be than a new person living on the earth?

Daily Challenge

Talk about your openness as a couple to children. Discuss your thoughts with your spouse and be honest about any fears, concerns, or desires. Do you have a common desire in family size? Do you believe that God will provide for your needs?

Prayer

Lord, teach me to be generous.
Teach me to serve you as you deserve;
to give and not to count the cost,
to fight and not to heed the wounds,
to toil and not to seek for rest,
to labor and not to ask for reward,
save that of knowing that I do your will.[3]

---

3. Attributed to Saint Ignatius of Loyola. "A Mysterious Ignatian Prayer," Thinking Faith, last updated February 17, 2012, http://www.thinkingfaith. org/articles/20120217_1.htm.

❧

Day Four

Trusting God, Even When It Hurts

Have you ever wanted to punch someone in the face because they said something mean or hurtful to you? Hopefully, you refrained from giving John (or Jane) Doe that black and blue shiner, but the comment may have wounded you more deeply than any punch to the face.

Someone we know experienced such a moment when an older Catholic coworker flippantly (and rudely) remarked that our friend still didn't have children after being married for nine months. Our friend comes from a very large family, and while she and her husband had been trying to conceive, they hadn't yet succeeded. The coworker's comment stung not only because she was assuming that the couple was not open to life, but also because our friends really wanted children. Some of you reading this devotional may have experienced this painful ache for one year, ten years, or even your whole marriage.

The pain of infertility is an often unspoken, agonizing reality for many couples. It's tempting to give in to thoughts of anger or disappointment directed against our own bodies. Men and women may feel broken or flawed and personally responsible, bearing all the weight of infertility upon their shoulders. Emotions can range from anger to frustration to sorrow, and we can experience a time of darkness, feeling as if God has abandoned us.

It's a great mystery why many faith-filled couples experience infertility. When so many children are aborted or abandoned on a daily basis, why would God allow couples that *desire* children to go without?

While we may never find the answer to that question here on this earth, a few things can be said to those who have experienced infertility in their marriage.

First, your pain and your ache are absolutely valid. If you read yesterday's reflection, you know why. Children are a blessing and a gift. Infertility wouldn't hurt so much if this weren't true. Comments telling you to "cheer you up" or to "enjoy your alone time" with your spouse or that "you should adopt" will never make the ache go away.

Secondly, know that your marriage can still absolutely bear glorious fruit, because love *always* bears fruit. Your love for Jesus as his disciple will bear the fruits of the Spirit. Your love for your spouse will bear those fruits, as well. And your marriage will be fruitful for every person you meet. A couple very dear to us was never able to have children, but because of their involvement in youth ministry and the number of lives they changed, many have called them "mom and dad." Their marriage has borne the fruits of love, joy, peace, patience, kindness, generosity, faithfulness, gentleness, self-control (see Gal 5:22-23). They are truly witnesses of a marriage that has endured great suffering and yet is filled with gratitude and rejoicing rather than of resentment and despair.

Lastly, no matter what suffering we have experienced in this life, God calls us to trust him through the trials and the pain. For anyone who has suffered, this is easier said than done. But, again, we have a Savior who showed us the way—he who trusted in his Father's plans, even when it meant his death. And we have a mother in Our Lady who trusted God's plans even when it meant the death of her Son.

With God, light can come from darkness. Healing can come from pain. Strength can come from weakness and suffering. Let us let God into our darkness, pain, and suffering—when we do, he will shine light and healing on the ache of the longing for children and allow us to be more fruitful than we could ever imagine through our witness of love.

Daily Challenge

Reflect on this passage:

But [the Lord] said to me, "My grace is sufficient for you, for power is made perfect in weakness.' So, I will boast all the more gladly of my weaknesses, so that the power of Christ may dwell in me. Therefore I am content with weaknesses, insults, hardships, persecutions, and calamities for the sake of Christ; for whenever I am weak, then I am strong" (2 Cor 12:9).

Prayer

Lord, help us to pray the simple prayer of Saint Faustina: *Jesus, I trust in you.* May we trust you in times of joy and consolation, and in times of suffering and sadness. Jesus, you alone are all we need.

☙

DAY FIVE

The Family's Mission in the World

The family has a mission, should we choose to accept it.

Understanding the many challenges the family faces in the modern world, Saint John Paul II wrote an eloquent text called *The Role of the Christian Family in the Modern World*, that particularly encouraged young people setting out on the great adventure of marriage and family. In it, John Paul II shares that God not only forms the identity of the family but also our mission: "Each family finds within itself a summons that cannot be ignored, and that specifies both its dignity and its responsibility: family, *become* what you *are*."[4]

What *are* we?

John Paul II goes on to clarify by saying that we must become more and more "a community of life and love" that lives the mission "to guard, reveal, and communicate love."[5]

Rather than through extraordinary, feats of great sacrifice, we live this mission of the family in the hundreds of little (often hidden) moments. From getting up early to feed a baby, doing chores without complaint, and welcoming inconveniences as

---

4. The Role of the Christian Family in the Modern World (*Familiaris Consortio*) (Boston: St. Paul Editions, 1982), no. 17.

5. Ibid.

small opportunities of love, these are the moments of mission for family. In these moments we learn the truth of what Saint Teresa of Kolkata often emphasized: that while not all of us can do great things, we can *all* do little things with great love.

Most of us already know how easy it is to fail in this mission. Family members can rub each other the wrong way; we can get snippy or short-tempered, or even blow up in anger. If we have children, we may neglect our spouse because so much energy has been spent (or sucked out of us) by our kids. We can shut out our bigger responsibilities to society by turning our backs on things that we feel don't concern us.

But John Paul II encourages us to do otherwise: "Since the Creator of all things has established the conjugal partnership as the beginning and basis of human society," the family is "the first and vital cell of society."[6] Most of us will lead quiet lives within our families, but you may also be called to live out your mission of love in service to the local community or as a member of a governing body. If the Christian message of love truly is "the Good News," we cannot be afraid to share it with a world starving for real love.

How we love one another as a family matters, and it is a witness to the world. Even in our failures, we stretch and grow and learn how to love one another better. We build up one another and thus build up the Kingdom of God here on earth.

---

6. Ibid., no. 42.

Daily Challenge

Discuss how you think God might be stretching you as a family (or future family) to serve the world. Perhaps it's by getting more involved in your parish, serving the poor, or mentoring another couple in their relationship.

Prayer

Lord, give us the courage to embrace whatever mission you entrust to our family. Help us to bear daily challenges with acceptance and joy so that we can be better models of sacrificial love.

༄

DAY SIX

Family and Forgiveness

> [Mercy is] the movement of the heart (*cor*) that is shaken at the sight of another's plight (*miseria*) and moves to do something, going out of itself toward the other.[7]

Preparing for Thanksgiving, Christmas, or any family gathering can be stressful. There's food to be cooked, cleaning to be done, and gifts to be bought. Family gatherings can also give rise to many conflicting emotions: excitement, fear, dread, annoyance, anger, disappointment, and tenderness are just some of the possibilities. Sometimes we experience all of these in one evening!

We all know from experience that no family is perfect. We hurt one another by our words and actions. None of us is perfect. We all come from a wounded and sinful human family. Our wounded nature plays out in family dynamics that can easily be strained, and bitterness can run deep. Holding grudges and refusing to forgive one another often tears families apart.

Some of us may have to forgive family members who have said hurtful things, whether it was a careless comment said by your sibling or constant verbal abuse from a parent or family

---

7. Erasmo Leiva-Merikakis, *Fire of Mercy, Heart of the Word: Meditations on the Gospel According to Saint Matthew* (San Francisco: Ignatius Press, 1996), 197.

member. Others may have a deep wound from the effects of a physically abusive or even sexually abusive family member.

Forgiveness does not mean forgetting and giving those who have wronged us a free pass. What forgiveness does, however, is put salve on the wound, so it heals faster. When the Body of Christ is wounded and divided by sin, forgiveness is in effect a healing and reuniting of the Body of Christ. The hope is that both parties would reach across the divide to come together and experience the strength of mercy over sin and pettiness. However, even if it is only *one* person who chooses to forgive or even say "sorry" (if you were the offender), God's mercy and grace still comes into the situation and has the power to change hearts. But we must first be willing to open up our own hearts and be cleansed of bitterness and hate.

The *Catechism of the Catholic Church* has some amazing words on forgiveness:

> Now—and this is daunting—this outpouring of [God's] mercy cannot penetrate our hearts as long as we have not forgiven those who have trespassed against us. Love, like the Body of Christ, is indivisible; we cannot love the God we cannot see if we do not love the brother or sister we do see. In refusing to forgive our brothers and sisters, our hearts are closed and their hardness makes them impervious to the Father's merciful love; but in confessing our sins, our hearts are opened to his grace. (*CCC* 2840)

As we seek to be the hands and feet of Christ in the world, we must have enough humility to accept that, by our own power, we can't heal all wounds. Christ the divine healer can repair and bring about a full healing of divisions, including those within our families, but it's always in his own way and time, not ours.

Forgiveness shows that love is stronger than sin—or even death. May we be so bold as to forgive and offer up to God any hurts we have been holding onto. May we be merciful to others because God has already been so merciful with us: "Blessed are the merciful, for they will be shown mercy" (Mt 5:7).

Daily Challenge

Pray for your family and consider all who have been hurt or note where there are divisions. Share these with your spouse. If possible, what can you both do to bring about healing?

Prayer

Our Father, who art in heaven,
hallowed be thy name;
Thy kingdom come;
Thy will be done on earth as it is in heaven.
Give us this day our daily bread,
and forgive us our trespasses,
as we forgive those who trespass against us,
and lead us not into temptation,
but deliver us from evil. Amen.

❧

DAY SEVEN

Reunion with the Trinity

Whether with family, friends, or old classmates, reunions can be great fun. We see faces we haven't seen in years, swap stories, share about our new families, and rehash nostalgic stories. With the rise of social media, the necessity of physical gatherings (particularly high school reunions) has declined, but that doesn't negate the power of seeing our loved ones again.

Life in heaven, also called the *eschaton* or the beatific vision, "is beyond all understanding and description" (*CCC* 1027). But we all have a standing invitation to this union with Christ and through Christ. Every Sunday in our Creed we state our belief in the "resurrection of the body," an actual event by which we will be blessed to receive *our bodies* again.

Saint John Paul II shares, "This will be a completely new experience.... The man of the 'future world' will find in this new experience of his own body *the fulfillment* of what he carried in himself perennially and historically" (*TOB* 69:5).

The human person is a union of body and soul, so we aren't fully human unless our souls and our bodies are one. When the body dies, the soul lives on, but we are not fully a human person until we are reunited with our bodies. In other words, we won't be fully ourselves until our souls are reunited with our bodies at the final resurrection. There are currently only *two* physical human bodies in heaven—Jesus Christ and our Mother Mary.

Have you ever thought about this? (When we teach the theology of the body to young people, this fact often blows their minds.) The ascension of Christ and the assumption of Mary are not dry dogma or questions on a theology exam, but *living realities* that should move us to awe and wonder.

With Mary and all the angels and saints, heaven will not be boring. Heaven will be a radiant explosion of dynamic love. Heaven will be a place of divine *ecstasy*—a literal *going out* of ourselves in an active exchange of communion. Heaven will be a coming home.

It may be confusing then that Christ tells his disciples that "in the resurrection they neither marry nor are given in marriage (Mt 22:30). But we needn't fear. Marriage has existed from the beginning to point us to the Trinity. When we arrive at the shores of eternity, we will no longer need marriage to be our directional map because we will have arrived at our destination! What's more, we will be *more unified* in heaven than we could ever be on earth. Our love will not end in heaven but be perfected in the presence of the Trinity. In this "union of communion" (*TOB* 68:4) we will be seen by all and see all.

We are called to a reunion with the Trinity where we will be united with the Father who created us, the Son who saves us, and the Holy Spirit who sanctifies us. In heaven, we will experience happiness beyond anything we have tasted on earth. The Church longs "to be united with Christ, her Bridegroom, in the glory of heaven" where she "will rejoice one day with [her] Beloved, in a happiness and rapture that can never end" (*CCC*, 1821).

Come, Lord Jesus!

Daily Challenge

Discuss any graces you have received over the past six weeks while learning and praying with Saint John Paul II and his theology of the body. How has your understanding of heaven and God's love changed? Do you know anyone else in your life who should hear this message?

Prayer

What no eye has seen, nor ear heard,
nor the human heart conceived,
what God has prepared for those who love him.

1 Corinthians 2:9

Afterword

On October 18, 2015, Louis and Zélie Martin, the parents of the beloved Saint Thérèse of Lisieux, became canonized saints in the Catholic Church. It was a historic event because for the first time in history the Church canonized a married couple together *at the same time*.

These two weren't recognized as saints just because they raised awesome kids. (Out of nine children, five survived to adulthood and they all became nuns!) No one is born a saint. Louis and Zélie understood that holiness consisted in offering themselves daily to Christ and allowing him to slowly transform them from the inside out. What this humble couple has shown to the world is that the graces God desires to pour out are not limited to priests and nuns, but are available to *all the faithful*, including those called to the sacred vocation of marriage.

It was Louis and Zélie's lived example of simplicity, devotion to one another, and fidelity in always putting God first that sanctified their marriage and eventually their children. They lived *the spousal meaning of the body* before Saint John Paul II ever coined the phrase. It is providential that the Church has elevated this powerful couple as a witness of holy matrimony at a time when marriage in our culture faces serious struggles.

This saintly couple can answer the question you may now have: Where do we go from here?

We hope you have grown in a general understanding of what John Paul II taught in his profound catechesis on the dignity of the body and human sexuality. We hope you've learned more about authentic love, and how the vows and promises we make on our wedding day provide a roadmap to love our spouse freely, totally, faithfully, and fruitfully.

We also hope that you've grown in greater knowledge of the gift of your spouse and maybe even had a few laughs along the way. There is so much more that can be said about the theology of the body, and thankfully many other scholars, speakers, and writers continue to plumb its depths. It reinvigorated our faith and we hope it does the same for you.

In striving to live a joy-filled and holy marriage, there are also many married saints to whom we can look as models and ask for prayers. Mary and Joseph are the married couple *par excellence* that we can invoke for guidance and powerful intercession. While not much is written about Saint Joachim and Anne (the parents of Mary), we know that they were also devout and faithful to the call of the Lord. Saint Cecilia, patron of musicians, was married and, inspired by her example of great faith, her husband converted to Christianity. Saint Thomas More endured great persecution and his eventual death in England with the steadfast support of his wife and children. And, of course, Saint Louis and

Zélie are our modern witnesses of joyful marriage even through the trials of war, poverty, and tragic illness.

You have no doubt witnessed some holy marriages yourself. Maybe you've been inspired by your parents, grandparents, or another couple you have encountered. *Your marriage* can also be a holy marriage. Through loving one another, dancing with one another, serving the poor or going on mission trips together, you can witness to the next generation that marriage is not the end of anything but a beautiful adventure of love that can bear great fruit for the world.

The fact that our marriage has been called to be a physical sign here on earth is a great call and a great responsibility. We were created to live forever in communion with the God who loves us, and this fact is written right into our bodies. God calls us to live this truth in our marriages. We must be missionaries who live our marriages joyfully so that the world can see this good news.

The Eucharist is the food for our journey. We cannot achieve holiness on our own, but in and through Jesus Christ, the Spouse who calls us all to the heavenly marriage feast. *"This is my body given up for you."* Each husband and wife should say this every day to one another, as we also receive the gift of Christ's Body to nourish us while on this earthly pilgrimage.

Remember, you were created to be a gift to the world—now go be a gift to your spouse!

Saint Joseph and Mary Most Holy, *pray for us*!
Saints Louis and Zélie Martin, *pray for us*!
Saint John Paul II, *pray for us*!

Appendix I

Recommended Reading

The richness of Saint John Paul II's vision of the theology of the body is vast, and many other authors have already written great works of varying scope. Here are some recommended readings to dive deeper into this treasure trove, as well as some complementary books and documents we've read that have helped us to "flesh out" the great mystery of our bodily love in the divine image.

On Marriage

Evert, Jason. *How to Find Your Soulmate Without Losing Your Soul.* San Diego: Totus Tuus Press, 2011.

John Paul II. *Man and Woman He Created Them: A Theology of the Body.* Boston: Pauline Books & Media, 2006.

Lewis, C. S. *The Four Loves.* New York: Mariner Books, 2012.

Sheen, Fulton. *Three to Get Married.* New York: Scepter Publications, Inc., 1992.

Sri, Edward. *Men, Women, and the Mystery of Love.* Cincinnati: Servant Books, 2007.

West, Christopher. *Theology of the Body for Beginners: A Basic Introduction to Pope John Paul II's Sexual Revolution*. West Chester: Ascension Press, 2009.

Papal Documents

Benedict XVI. *Deus Caritas Est* [On Christian Love]. Vatican Web site. December 25, 2005. Accessed Nov. 3, 2016. http://w2.vatican.va/content/benedict-xvi/en/encyclicals/documents/hf_ben-xvi_enc_20051225_deus-caritas-est.html.

Francis. *Amoris Laetitia* [On Love in the Family]. Vatican Web site. March 19, 2016. Accessed Nov, 3, 2016. http://w2.vatican.va/content/francesco/en/apost_exhortations/documents/papa-francesco_esortazione-ap_20160319_amoris-laetitia.html.

John Paul II. *Familiaris Consortio* [On the Role of the Christian Family in the Modern World]. Vatican Web site. Nov. 22, 1981. Accessed Nov. 3, 2016. http://w2.vatican.va/content/john-paul-ii/en/apost_exhortations/documents/hf_jp-ii_exh_19811122_familiaris-consortio.html.

———.*Mulieris Dignitatem* [On the Dignity and Vocation of Women]. Vatican Web site. August 15, 1988. Accessed Nov. 3, 2016. http://w2.vatican.va/content/john-paul-ii/en/apost_letters/1988/documents/hf_jp-ii_apl_19880815_mulieris-dignitatem.html.

On Sexuality

Bachiochi, Erika. *Women, Sex and the Church: A Case for Catholic Teaching*. Boston: Pauline Books & Media, 2010.

Dimech-Juchniewicz, Jean and Paul A. Carpentier. *Facing Infertility: A Catholic Approach*. Boston: Pauline Books & Media, 2012.

Fisher, Simcha. *The Sinner's Guide to Natural Family Planning*. Huntington: Our Sunday Visitor, 2014.

Franks, Angela. *Contraception and Catholicism: What the Church Teaches and Why*. Boston: Pauline Books & Media, 2013.

West, Christopher. *Good News About Sex and Marriage: Honest questions and answers about Catholic teaching*. Ann Arbor: Servant Publications, 2000.

On Parenting

Cardaronella, Marc. *Keep Your Kids Catholic: Sharing Your Faith and Making It Stick*. Notre Dame: Ave Maria Press, 2016.

Guarendi, Ray. *Discipline That Lasts a Lifetime: The Best Gift You Can Give Your Kids*. Ann Arbor: Servant Publications, 2003.

Popcak, Greg and Lisa. *Beyond the Birds and the Bees*. West Chester: Ascension Press, 2012.

———. *Parenting with Grace: The Catholic Parents' Guide to Raising almost Perfect Kids*. Huntington: Our Sunday Visitor, 2010.

On Overcoming Pornography

Fradd, Matt. *Delivered: True Stories of Men and Women Who Turned from Porn to Purity*. San Diego: Catholic Answers Press, 2013.

LeJeune, Marcel. *Cleansed: A Catholic Guide to Freedom from Porn*. Boston: Pauline Books & Media, 2016.

APPENDIX II

On Natural Family Planning (NFP)

Natural Family Planning (NFP) is a general name for the natural, scientific, and moral methods of family planning that chart the fertility cycle of a woman to determine when a pregnancy could occur. NFP is *not* the outdated rhythm method, mere guesswork, or some form of strange witchcraft. It's *real science* that requires that the couple track the woman's biorhythms and then communicate about their intentions: *Are we ready to have a child? Should we abstain right now?*

We benefit today from advances in science that give us natural (organic!) methods to help couples either achieve or avoid pregnancies without artificial barriers. The natural signs of fertile or infertile phases in a woman's cycle (mucus color, consistency, etc.) are monitored and assessed. NFP then demands something of a couple that these days may seem extraordinary—self-control. If a couple desires to avoid pregnancy, they abstain from sex on fertile days; if a couple desires a child, they target the fertile days.

The man thus learns a deeper respect for the woman's body and is less likely to view his wife as a sexual object to be sterilized with a pill or artificial device. What's more, NFP can help women with irregular cycles or even unearth, with the help of Natural Procreative Technology (NaPro), the root cause of infertility.

There are a variety of models of NFP that vary in their techniques or demands on the couple, the current best being the Creighton model, the Billings Ovulation method, and the Sympto-Thermal method.

What does it take to effectively practice NFP? Communication, self-control (depending on your hope of either having three kids or thirty kids), patience, mutual self-sacrificial love, and openness to God's plan. NFP isn't "Catholic Contraception" because, by its very nature, it is open to God's will and doesn't artificially manipulate the gift of fertility or attempt to extinguish it altogether. Every sexual union between a husband and wife is a fundamentally open, life-giving action. Even if the couple were trying to actively avoid pregnancy, they still understand that an unexpected child is a gift to be received and not a "mistake" to be dealt with.

Couples who effectively practice NFP boast of an average of ninety-eight percent effective rates (if the rules are followed) and lower-than-average divorce rates.

If it sounds daunting or overly technical, don't worry. Many good mentors and instructors now help couples learn NFP. Your local parish or diocesan office will be able to guide you to the proper resources.

While all this may seem scary, NFP actually frees couples to abandon their lives into the loving hands of God. Couples who reject NFP as too much hassle or see it as a burden to exercise self-control will often find the call of marriage itself to be too demanding. Since the methods of NFP respect the love-giving (unitive) and life-giving (procreative) nature of the conjugal act, the couple naturally grows in communication, respect, and intimacy, fulfilling God's beautiful design for married love!

BOOKS & MEDIA

The Daughters of St. Paul operate book and media centers at the following addresses. Visit, call, or write the one nearest you today, or find us at www.paulinestore.org.

CALIFORNIA

3908 Sepulveda Blvd, Culver City, CA 90230	310-397-8676
3250 Middlefield Road, Menlo Park, CA 94025	650-369-4230

FLORIDA

145 S.W. 107th Avenue, Miami, FL 33174	305-559-6715

HAWAII

1143 Bishop Street, Honolulu, HI 96813	808-521-2731

ILLINOIS

172 North Michigan Avenue, Chicago, IL 60601	312-346-4228

LOUISIANA

4403 Veterans Memorial Blvd, Metairie, LA 70006	504-887-7631

MASSACHUSETTS

885 Providence Hwy, Dedham, MA 02026	781-326-5385

MISSOURI

9804 Watson Road, St. Louis, MO 63126	314-965-3512

NEW YORK

115 E. 29th Street, New York City, NY 10016	212-754-1110

SOUTH CAROLINA

243 King Street, Charleston, SC 29401	843-577-0175

TEXAS

Currently no book center; for parish exhibits or outreach evangelization, contact: 210-569-0500, or SanAntonio@paulinemedia.com, or P.O. Box 761416, San Antonio, TX 78245

VIRGINIA

1025 King Street, Alexandria, VA 22314	703-549-3806

CANADA

3022 Dufferin Street, Toronto, ON M6B 3T5	416-781-9131

¡También somos su fuente para libros,
videos y música en español!